Bang

The Strength to Succeed

Contents

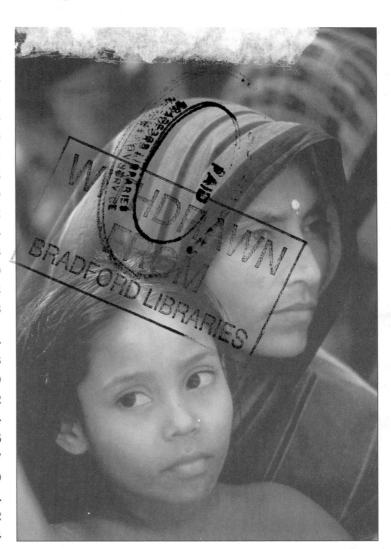

Designed by Oxfam Design Department 97/MCA/95
Published and printed by Oxfam,
274 Banbury Road, Oxford OX2 7DZ, UK
ISBN 0 85598 328 0
(first edition ISBN 0 85598 127 X)

Jim Monan

NICK FOGDEN

**Transplanting rice
seedlings.**

2

Introduction

The people of Bangladesh have a past history which would have broken the spirit and will of a weaker society. Exploited down the centuries by Moghuls, Britons, and Pakistanis, and more recently by repressive governments of their own, they have survived with a doggedness and cheerfulness that are a testimony to their strength and endurance.

As if the yoke of human oppression were not enough, the climate (assisted by human activities) has also conspired against them. During the decade 1984–1994 they have been visited by natural disasters of varying types and magnitude: a cyclone in the Bay of Bengal in April 1991 killed over 138,000 people and rendered millions homeless; in September of the same year a flood destroyed tens of thousands of hectares of crops; in 1994, another devastating cyclone struck. Five times in ten years, major floods have brought the country to a standstill.

The recurrent disasters have provided the Western world with a standard image of the Bangladeshi: a picture of a downtrodden individual who annually buckles under a major flood or cyclone. The negative images which appear in the Western media are generally selected to reinforce this depressing view. Nothing could be further from the truth.

The other image which the discerning observer will recognise is that of a people full of courage and resilience in dealing with situations which would leave most Westerners in total despair. The pages which follow are a tribute to the people of Bangladesh for demonstrating to us the heights of bravery and skill which humankind is capable of in the extremes of adversity. For that we owe them not only our sympathy and assistance when disaster strikes but also our admiration for the way in which they triumphantly overcome their difficulties.

After the 1991 cyclone, Bay of Bengal.

SHAHIDUL ALAM

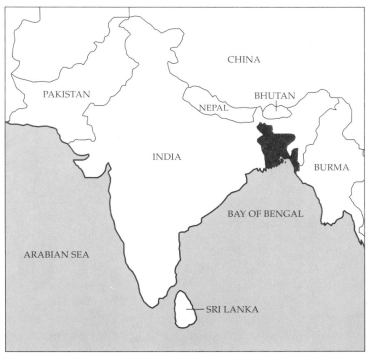

3

Physical features

Bangladesh is the largest delta in the world and, apart from a few small hills in the north and south-east, is flat as far as the eye can see. Very little of the country is more than 40 feet above sea level. In a normal monsoon, one third of its 22 million acres of cultivated land is flooded.

Three major river systems and their countless tributaries and distributaries form the delta. The Ganges, Brahmaputra, and the lesser Meghna rivers pour out of the mountains to the north and flow through Bangladesh to reach the sea in the Bay of Bengal. With them they bring millions of cubic feet of snowmelt. This, added to the monsoon rainfall, which can be as great as 250 centimetres in some areas, results in a vast amount of water which can be as devastating as it is bountiful.

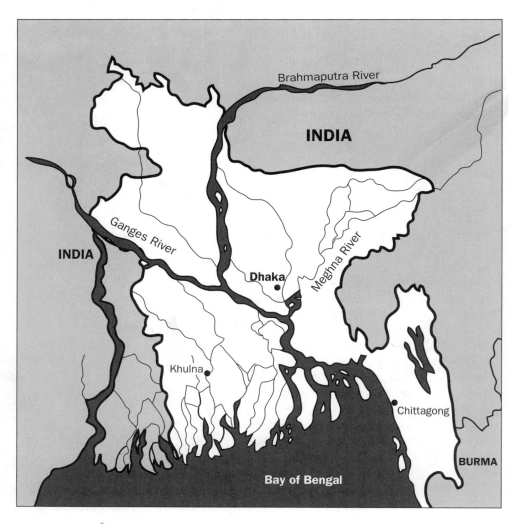

These great rivers also bring with them rich alluvial materials which they deposit as silt to form what is recognised to be potentially some of the most productive agricultural land in the world.

Bangladesh is an agricultural country with the vast majority of people involved in food production. Rice is grown during the rainy season and, where irrigation is available, a second, dry-season rice crop is possible; wheat and vegetables are cultivated in the short, dry winter from November to February. In the low hills to the north-east, tea and some coffee is grown. The other main crop is jute, which gives the strong natural fibre used in the carpet and sacking industries. Bangladesh is the leading world producer.

Fisheries off the coast and along the rivers are another natural resource. A vast quantity of natural gas lies beneath the rich alluvial swamp that characterises so much of the country. Although some oil deposits have been found there is no indication as yet of their potential.

Almost 80 per cent of Bangladeshis live in rural areas.

Fisheries, coastal and inland, are a valuable natural resource.

TANVIR

(below) **A little girl feeding her ducklings on a flooded paddy-field.**

SHAHIDUL ALAM

Urban life

There are only three cities of any size: Dhaka, the capital, situated in the centre of the country, has a population of about 7.2 million; Chittagong, the large port in the south-east on the Bay of Bengal, has around 2.4 million; Khulna, the other port in the south-west, has just under 1 million inhabitants. Apart from these three cities, and the 'education town' of Rajshahi, Bangladesh is primarily a country of villages; conservative estimates put the number at over 70,000.

Bangladesh shares with many developing countries a major problem: that of rapid urbanisation. The rural population is being forced to the cities to seek employment, at a rate, according to UN estimates, of about five per cent per annum. Projections suggest urban dwellers will grow from approximately 20 per cent of the population now to 25 per cent by the year 2001, which means an urban population of between 30 and 35 million. This will present an enormous challenge for government and non-government sectors alike if the chronic social deprivation associated with urban slums is to be avoided.

(far left) **Old houses in Dhaka**

(below) **When poor rural people move to the cities to look for work, they are often forced to live in appalling conditions.**

WALTER HOLT

Colonial history

The rich agricultural land of the delta has been attractive to colonial exploiters down the centuries. Bengal was first colonised by the Turko-Afghan rulers of northern India in the thirteenth century. They brought with them the religion of Islam and expertise in weaving, and developed a high quality muslin industry.

The next wave of colonists were the Moghuls in the sixteenth century, who added Bengal to their north Indian empire and made Dhaka the capital of that part of their domain. The Moghuls did little to change the status quo, but with the arrival of the British in the eighteenth century, far-reaching changes were instituted. To protect the developing British textile industry the export of Bengali cotton and muslin was banned. This ban virtually destroyed a thriving rural industry and brought destitution to the weavers.

The Raj introduced the concept of 'permanent settlement', imposed heavy taxation on land and decreed that it could be bought and sold, something that had hitherto been unknown. In East Bengal, the new taxes forced the sale of many large estates to wealthy Hindus, who became known as *zamindars,* who set rents on land tilled by peasants, to pay

Dates and events

4th century AD	Gupta Empire established in northern India and Hinduism spreads eastwards to Bengal.
8th century	Invaders from the Arabian peninsula bring Islam to the Sind (now part of Pakistan).
12th century	Islamic Empire established with its capital in Delhi. Hindu states subordinate to the Turkish-influenced rulers in Delhi.
1526	Moghul Empire established under Babur, stretching from Afghanistan to Bihar.
1555	Akbar succeeds Babur and the empire is expanded to include Bengal. Islamic influence grows.
1600	First British East India Company formed.
1639	Fort St George established at Madras as the first territory of British India.
1696	Fort William, near Calcutta, founded as British military and trading post.
1707	Moghul Empire disintegrates into group of princely states.
1757	Clive defeats Nawab of Bengal at the Battle of Plassey.
1764	British East India Company takes over authority for administration of the whole of Bengal.
1770	Famine kills 10 million people in Bengal.
1789	Lord Cornwallis changes land tenure system from stewardship to ownership. New landowners are Hindu *zamindars* who collect taxes for the British.
1859	'Indigo riots' when peasant farmers object to British control of what they grow.
1905	Bengal partitioned into Muslim east, Hindu west. Muslim League formed, 1906.
1911	Bengal reunited after Hindu pressure.
1947	Independence and Partition. Bengal split into East Pakistan and West Bengal, which remains part of India.
1971	War of Liberation and foundation of new state of Bangladesh.

the taxes levied by the British. The rents were often too high for peasant farmers to meet and they were frequently dispossessed and forced off the land; this pattern of dispossession still continues today. The colonial masters also forced farmers to grow export cash-crops such as indigo, tea, jute, and opium (used in the exploitative trade with China). The result was food shortages and riots.

The Raj encouraged political activity as long as it was based on religion. This kept Hindu *zamindars* and their supporters at loggerheads with Muslim peasant farmers, and the divided population was easier to rule. The religious divisions played a major part in the history of the area in the first half of this century. For a few years, Bengal was split up into Muslim East and Hindu West, and it was at this time that the Muslim League came into being. The League was to figure continuously in the nationalist struggle, arguing for independence for Muslim areas.

When the British finally left in 1947, the Partition settlement resulted in East Bengal becoming East Pakistan by virtue of its Muslim majority while West Bengal, despite having the same language, traditions, and culture, became a part of India. Pakistan was a country in two halves, hundreds of miles apart.

The new dispensation brought more exploitation for the Bengalis, this time by their own countrymen. West Pakistan kept East Pakistan in economic subservience and refused to grant Bengali the status of a national language. Throughout the 1960s the East Pakistan opposition harassed the government. The nationalist cause was identified with a political party, the Awami League, led by Sheikh Mujibur Rahman.

In the 1970 election, the Awami League won a majority of seats but was not allowed to form a government. The West instituted a military campaign against the East and the 'War of Liberation' had begun. Millions of people fled to India to escape the carnage. The West Pakistan armed forces, with a philosophy of racial superiority and with vastly superior military technology, killed around two million Bengalis. In late 1971 the Indian government, burdened by the millions of refugees encamped in West Bengal, perhaps wishing to give Pakistan a military lesson, and no doubt for their own political reasons, decided to intervene, and Pakistan soon surrendered. On 16 December 1971, Bangladesh came into being.

PENNY TWEEDIE

A family emerges from hiding during the War of Independence, December 1971.

Political struggles

The short history of Bangladesh has been one of political turmoil and upheaval. Two of its presidents have been assassinated and there have been periods of martial law and states of emergency, with large-scale imprisonment of political prisoners. Frequent strikes and demonstrations remind politicians and military rulers that people demand to be consulted at whatever cost.

Sheikh Mujib, who led the country in the War of Liberation, became the new nation's first Prime Minister but his Awami League government proved inefficient and corrupt. A famine in 1974, when warehouses were full of grain because of stock-piling by merchants, was the beginning of the end for Mujib. In August 1975 he was murdered by the military. After four changes of government in a few months, Major General Ziaur Rahman came to power. He proved to be popular among the peasantry and ruled as a soldier until early 1977 when he declared himself President.

After a brief rule, President Ziaur Rahman was also assassinated, in May 1981. The assassin, General Manzur, believed he was taking part in an army plot but in turn was gunned down by other army officers. This dark episode in the history of the young nation has never been satisfactorily explained. Less than a year later, another general, H.M. Ershad, seized control in a bloodless coup.

Ershad faced many challenges to his leadership. There were frequent strikes and demonstrations, sometimes violent, protesting against martial law and poor working conditions. Ershad banned political activity, and opposition leaders were, on occasions, put under house arrest. Ershad wanted a constitutional role for the military, knowing he could not rule without their support.

In November 1990 Ershad could no longer convince the people that he was the man to lead Bangladesh. Mass demonstrations against him took place all over the country and eventually the military refused to act against the demonstrators. After eight years of ruling Bangladesh, partly under martial law and latterly as a presidential dictator, Ershad fell from power. The people of Bangladesh had triumphed against autocracy and Ershad was tried for corruption, and given a prison sentence.

In February 1991 the first truly democratic elections for almost a decade brought success for the Bangladesh Nationalist Party (BNP) led by the widow of the late President Ziaur Rahman. She formed a government in temporary alliance with the Jamaat-e-Islam (an Islamic religious party) and through the appointment of 30 women to specially reserved places in the parliament. The main opposition party is the Awami League, led by the daughter of the late President Mujib, the founding father of Bangladesh.

The electorate demonstrated its independence in local elections in January 1993. Three million voters in the major cities rejected the ruling Bangladesh National Party and in both Dhaka and Chittagong returned mayors from the Awami League. Although some violence did occur in Dhaka as a result of the rejection of Khaleda Zia's party it did not undermine the process or result, and democracy, a young and fragile growth, continues to function.

The history of these turbulent years is all the more poignant when one remembers the millions who died in the

struggle to bring the country into existence. All that expenditure of human energy, courage, and ability represents an irreplaceable loss to the republic. Although much of the early idealism of the War of Liberation was dissipated in political squabbles and power struggles, democracy has eventually triumphed. In the long fight for justice and political freedom, the people of Bangladesh have proved that a commitment to the rights of a democratic society can overcome tyranny.

Democracy in Bangladesh

Bangladesh has a single chamber parliament which is elected under a universal adult franchise. There are 300 seats for elected members, and 30 reserved for selected women. Executive power is vested in the Prime Minister who appoints a Council of Ministers. The constitution provides for a President who is indirectly elected by parliament. Laws are enacted by a simple majority but constitutional amendments require a two-thirds majority. The parliamentary term is for five years, unless dissolved by the President.

The constitution states that the judiciary should be independent, but under a Constitutional Amendment enacted in 1975 the appointment of judges to the high court is in the power of the President and not the Chief Justice. It is difficult to see how the judges can be independent if the President can hire and fire them at will; and since the ruling

Sheikh Mujib, the first Prime Minister of Bangladesh, at the height of his popularity shortly afer the War of Liberation, surrounded by cheering crowds.

11

party selects the President, it presumably can influence his decisions.

Local representative government is not well developed in the rural areas. There are elections for the chair and membership of a Union Parishad, covering between fifteen and twenty villages (around 25,000 people). These are non-partisan, although influenced by the political parties. Union Parishads have been unable to challenge the domination of central government on most issues. The local district administrations are not democratically accountable in any way.

Reserved seats for women?

Some feminists in Bangladesh, while supporting discrimination in favour of women's representation in parliament, believe it should not be on the basis of selection by the majority party. Not only is selection open to abuse, but it is ultimately demeaning to women who enter politics, implying that they are only in parliament thanks to the patronage of predominantly male political parties.

They believe that a better solution would be to have constituencies which could be contested only by women candidates. This might be a transitional phase until women contest parliamentary seats as equals with men. There are a few powerful women leaders in social and cultural institutions and NGOs who do not join political parties, and contest elections as independent candidates. Other women activists prefer to remain outside the political arena.

An independent woman

Hasnaara Begum is a development worker, supporting women's groups on Hatiya Island, in the Bay of Bengal. She has three children, and her husband is a guard at a bank. In 1992 she stood as an independent candidate for the Union council, the lowest tier of local government. It was the first time that a women had stood for election on Hatiya; a few years ago women were not even allowed to vote. Hasnaara was nominated by her women's group, who wanted her to represent their interests over problems such as dowry demands and violence against women.

Some of the men in the area were very opposed to the idea of a woman candidate. Some said 'How can we have a woman on the Union Council? Women's duties are to cook.'

Hasnaara Begum lost the election by only two votes. She intends to stand again in the next elections. 'I've learnt from experience. The votes were not counted properly; next time I'll make sure I'm involved in the counting, to see that it's fair.'

JOHN CLARK

Parliament building, Dhaka.

Land reform and poverty

An increase in the number of landless peasant farmers is one of the commonest problems in agricultural economies. Between the two great landmarks in the history of the area, Partition in 1947 and the War of Liberation in 1971, landlessness in Bangladesh increased from 15 per cent of the population to 37 per cent. At the present time the official figure is 62 per cent, although many observers would put it closer to 75 per cent.

Since Partition successive governments have framed legislation to break up large holdings and redistribute land to peasant farmers. This redistribution would also apply to large tracts of land owned by the government, estimated at 750,000 acres. In 1950 the Government of Pakistan proposed a Bill to abolish the *zamindary* (the wealthy, landlord class) and fix a ceiling of 33 acres per family. The landlords persuaded their friends in parliament to filibuster and then had so many dilution clauses inserted in the Bill that by the time it became a statute it was of no benefit to the landless.

After Liberation the ruling Awami League also proposed radical land reform and a better deal for sharecroppers, who had to give 50 per cent or more of a crop as a form of rent to the landowner. Again, the landed class exerted so much pressure that the Bill came to nothing.

When General Ziaur Rahman came to power he quickly became a champion of the peasantry, and the need for land reform was stressed by his Bangladesh National Party. This time there was international support in the powerful form of Robert Macnamara, then President of the World Bank, who stated publicly that if poor people were to sustain themselves they had to be given land. Unfortunately for the landless, the BNP's ranks were full of powerful landowners and once more the promises proved to be no more than hollow political slogans.

The proposals introduced by Ershad were comprehensive and radical:

- all *khas* land (government land to which no one has a title) should be distributed amongst the landless as quickly as possible
- sharecroppers should have legal protection and a just share of the crop grown on the land they cultivate
- the government should fix a daily minimum wage for agricultural labourers.

Ershad, apart from fixing the daily agricultural wage at 3.5 kilos of rice or its cash equivalent, failed to carry out significant land redistribution. Similarly, nothing has so far been done by the government of Khaleda Zia to redistribute *khas* land, and the issue does not even appear to be on the agenda. To those working with landless people, the silence of Khaleda Zia's government, and indeed that of the opposition parties, is deafening.

Can land reforms ever be carried out? Every country in Asia has a land reform programme but few governments have actually implemented them. Without the co-operation or coercion of powerful landowners, real land reform, involving the redistribution of large land-holdings, cannot happen. Yet the experiences of the Asian economic 'tigers' such as Taiwan and South Korea suggest it is a prerequisite of industrial development.

Land and power

In Bangladesh, political and economic power is largely based on control over land. This is as true today as it was during the period of the *zamindars* under the British Raj. What is different is the level of violence and corruption now associated with land ownership.

One widespread method used by rich landowners to take land from small cultivators is to forge land titles, then remove peasant farmers, claiming that the farmers' ancestors did not own the land or had mortgaged it to pay debts. Without accurate land-title records it is almost impossible for a poor cultivator to defend his claim. If he pursues an expensive court action he will almost certainly lose since the court, in the absence of land records, will find in favour of the rich and powerful, who often bribe the local administration.

On Hatiya Island in the Bay of Bengal an organisation called Dwip Unnayan Sangstha (DUS) estimates that there are 94,000 acres of cultivable land available. DUS reckons that if this *khas* land were distributed according to government rules every family would get 1.89 acres: more than enough to live on. Yet 60 per cent of the population is landless, having been driven off their plots by thugs working for large landowners.

On another island, Nizzumdwip, most of the inhabitants were killed by a cyclone in 1970. When the surviving relatives attempted to claim this *khas* land, *boro lok* (rich and powerful men) produced titles 'proving' that the dead families had sold the land to them. An even more sinister practice is to sell a forged land title to a third party who then forces the existing cultivator off the land. It is not uncommon for landowners who create forged land titles to sell the same piece of land to a number of unsuspecting small farmers.

Similar corrupt and violent methods are used against ethnic minorities who normally farm traditional land which has no written titles to it. By forging titles and bribing officials, landowners remove tribal people from land which has been farmed for centuries by their ancestors.

This Samata supporter's house was looted, cooking pots broken, and six months' rice supply stolen. Local landowners use various ways of intimidating people who stand up to them.

RO COLE

NGOs who work with the landless and small cultivators are having to change their strategies. Where previously their concern was to help landless people to gain titles to government-owned *khas* land, they now must try to address the whole issue of agrarian reform, which means understanding land surveys, land-title recording, and the complexities of land laws. The Association for Land Reform and Development (ALRD) believes that land reform is now a national issue which requires advocacy at the highest levels of government. ALRD provides the media with detailed information, and lobbies national institutions on the need for reform. It also organises training courses for the fieldworkers and officers of local NGOs working with the landless, covering the full range of agrarian reform issues, to equip them to provide para-legal services and information to small farmers forced into courts to fight for their land.

Samata's struggle

Samata is an organisation of landless men and women who live in the district of Pabna on the north bank of the Ganges. For the past ten years, they have been pressing claims for hundreds of acres of *khas* land in the areas around their villages. This land is farmed by rich and powerful individuals, who have no right to it but are supported by local authorities and police whom they bribe at regular intervals.

As Samata grew in organisational ability and confidence it was able to gain titles to redistributed land. As a result, it was subjected to harassment by police and other officials on behalf of the local elites, who saw Samata as an increasing threat. A number of false charges of rape, burglary, and even murder, have been brought against Samata members.

Sarwar is an elected member of the Samata executive. Speaking of a new murder charge against 36 members he said 'Previously we would have run away and gone into hiding when the authorities moved against us. Now we

Woman speaking at a Samata meeting. Pressing for land rights for women is part of Samata's strategy.

stay and fight for our rights.' Asked about his landlessness he explained that his father was a farmer with two acres of land who, when he discovered that Sarwar was a member of an organisation which helped the landless, disinherited him. According to Sarwar, his father is now 'one of the enemy'.

Anwara Begum is a woman in her forties, married to a landless labourer, and is proud to be a member of the Samata committee. In Bangladesh this is an unusual achievement for a woman. Although she is illiterate, she was selected by her fellow members to attend a conference in Calcutta. She said that Samata has now over 1,000 women members who will not give up the struggle until they get land.

Although Samata still suffers harassment at the hands of local officials and landowners, it achieved another notable victory for the landless in 1994. It 'won' about 400 acres of unused government land, on which it settled no fewer than 478 destitute families. It managed to secure leases from the local authority for permanent cultivation. This success was widely reported in the national press, and shows that even if the government remains silent on this crucial issue, landless people and their organisations will continue their struggle for rights.

SHAFIQUL ALAM

'If I had a little bit of land....'

Each year, thousands of families lose their land and homes to Bangladesh's powerful rivers, which are continually scouring land from one place and dumping it at another. Without land they often find it difficult to survive. If the family is headed by a woman, destitution may threaten unless a male relative is prepared to take them in.

Arfaza Begum came to the island of Nizzumdwip five years ago from neighbouring Hatiya, where she had to move three times as successive houses collapsed into the Meghna river. Her first husband used to get work building flood embankments, but he died of a diarrhoeal disease. They could not afford medical treatment for him. That was when Arfaza was 18: she was left with one son. Shortly afterwards the other villagers persuaded her to get married again, and she had a daughter, Jasmin, now aged eight. Her second husband died in 1988. Her son has married and moved away.

Arfaza Begum has a precarious existence as a squatter. Her tiny house with its palm-leaf walls and thatch roof stands on the bunds between two paddy fields. During the monsoon the waters come right up to her house and she has to wait for the floods to subside before she can go out.

'I heard that the government was allocating *khas* land here to people like us, so that's why I came from Hatiya. I thought I would be able to settle here, but they didn't allocate me any land because I'm a woman.

'I'm squatting here because I have nowhere else to go. I have to go round the neighbours every day asking for food. They usually give me something, a few taka or a handful of rice.

'Today I got a bar of soap and some rice from a family whose baby had just died. They asked me to pray for the child. My daughter and I are often hungry, she has to wait until I come home with something before she can eat.

'If I had a little bit of land, it would give me some security: I could have a kitchen garden and sell vegetables.'

Jainal Abedin belongs to one of Dwip Unnayan Sangstha's (DUS) community groups on Nizzumdwip. DUS helped Abedin and his wife, along with about 600 other families, to get two acres each of *khas* land registered in their names. Abedin and his family live in an attractive, tree-shaded village which they have named Chayabithi, which means Sharing. He showed us the family's land certificate, which carries photographs of him and his wife to show that the land is registered in both their names.

Like Arfaza Begum, Abedin used to live on Hatiya, and when his land was washed away 20 years ago he came to Nizzumdwip. Before his plot was legally allocated to him, he and his family were attacked by a landgrabber who did not live on Nizzumdwip but kept a large herd of cows there. The cows wandered freely and often damaged farmers' crops. When an angry farmer injured two of them in retaliation, the owner went to the police and accused Jainal Abedin of the crime.

'I was away fishing. The police came with the landgrabber and a lot of other men. They looted my house and threw my children out. My wife, who was seven months' pregnant, was beaten up with sticks. The neighbours took her to Hatiya hospital and luckily, apart from some cuts, she and the baby were all right. The police were waiting to arrest me when I got off the boat to come home. I was in prison for six weeks.'

The landgrabber deliberately prolonged the legal proceedings, so that the case dragged on for three years and cost Jainal Abedin 14,000 taka. DUS covered some of the costs and provided legal support. Eventually he was found innocent, and the people who gave false witness against him were imprisoned for ten days.

Home is a village called Sharing

SHAFIQUL ALAM

Jainal Abedin and his wife with their land certificate.

Poverty to prosperity

In 1983 a non-stock, non-profit organisation calling itself the Grameen Bank (it had existed since 1976 as a development credit project) came into being and started making small loans to very poor people to enable them to set up income-generating projects. By 1994 it had two million customers and had proved conclusively, by a repayment rate of over 95 per cent, that not only were the poor credit-worthy but that they could improve their own living situation if only those in control of the country's financial resources would trust them.

During the 1980s over 35,000 tubewells were sunk in the Bangladesh countryside to improve irrigation and agricultural production. Recently the Grameen Bank estimated that only ten per cent of them remained in good working condition. Officials saw the possibility of encouraging commercially-viable, diversified farms of around 50 acres, centred on a tubewell, which the Bank would maintain. The sharecroppers who farmed the land would buy the water from the Bank, which would negotiate a fair return for the sharecroppers from the landowners.

The Bank now has taken control of over 800 previously defective tubewells and has on average around 50 farming families operating a farm centred on each of these wells. The Bank offered incentives to farmers to grow other crops, such as maize, wheat and soya beans, as well as rice. The Bank provided seeds and technical assistance, and agreed to buy the crops at a fair price. To diversify further the Bank intends to help farmers to establish fish production, either by digging ponds, for which the Bank will provide credit, or growing fish during the rice season in the paddy fields. (This is possible because the farms do not use chemical fertilisers and pesticides, which would kill fish.)

Such innovations will not only give these small farmers a better income, but also improve the food security and nutrition of their families. Bangladesh as a whole may have much to learn from this Grameen Bank initiative. Because many countries now produce a surplus of rice, it is becoming less profitable to export it. Diversification of crops is necessary not only for better nutrition but also to compete with other nations in the region in the drive to export crops other than rice.

Masuda Khatun has done well with her savings. A member of a local women's group, she rears poultry, grows pumpkins and gourds, and has a cow and a calf.

SHAHIDUL ALAM

Banking on women

Out of the million borrowers of Grameen Bank, 92 per cent are women. Money directed to households via women proves to be much more fruitful than the same amount of capital directed to households via men. Women's income is used to the benefit of children and the household in general, and women have proved to be more responsible about the repayment of loans. Men, on the other hand, have different priorities; they are also more prone to defaulting on payments.

Giving priority to women did not come about smoothly. Much resistance manifested itself from husbands, religious leaders, and others. Moreover the bank had difficulty persuading the women themselves to borrow money, for they believed that they could not handle it by themselves. Persuaded by their culture and upbringing that they are weak, less useful to their families and society in general, women end up having very low self-esteem, which further marginalises them.

The Daily Star
Dhaka 21 November 1994

A carving put up by a family in memory of a dead relative.

Fighting for justice

Many women in Bangladesh villages have faced harassment from conservative religious forces or the vested interests of landlords, and in some cases, from a combination of both. Women who have taken loans from the Grameen Bank in an attempt to lift their families out of poverty have been pilloried by village *imams* who want to keep women in a position of subjugation. The work of the Grameen Bank has been condemned by conservative religious leaders as being 'against the will of God', in that it promotes a degree of emancipation and independence for poor women.

Women have even given their lives in the fight against corruption and the misuse of power. In the South Khulna area, where rich investors have taken over much of the agricultural land for shrimp production, the Bangladeshi NGO, Nijera Kori (We Shall Do It Ourselves) is currently fighting a court battle to bring to justice the murderers of one of its women members.

When a rich entrepreneur attempted to take over a local polder (agricultural land protected by an embankment) for shrimp cultivation the community, supported by Nijera Kori, refused to give over its only source of livelihood. The rich man responded by bringing in seven boat-loads of thugs to terrorise the local people. In a pitched battle 40 members of the community were badly injured and one brave Hindu woman called Karuna was murdered and her body taken away to prevent the police bringing a case.

The place where Karuna disappeared has now become a shrine for poor people and others who fight for justice. On 7 November each year they gather in their thousands to honour her memory. Even politicians from the major parties make speeches in her honour; but justice has yet to be done.

The influence of Islam

Although Bangladesh is a secular state, Islam as the state religion plays a prominent part in daily life. Yet as the election of Khaleda Zia demonstrates, Islamic conservatism is not the preferred option of the vast majority of the population. If it were, no woman would ever have reached the political heights of Khaleda Zia and the leader of the opposition, Sheikh Hasina. They may be rare exceptions in a society in which women are regarded as inferior to men; but they are, of course, the widow and daughter, respectively, of two of the previous leaders of Bangladesh.

Conservative Islam, however, exerts considerable pressure on the lives of ordinary Bangladeshis, out of all proportion to its numerical strength in the country and the tiny number of seats the Jamaat-e-Islam holds in parliament.

Many women in Bangladesh villages have experienced the power of conservative religious forces or landlords and in some cases a combination of both. Women who have taken loans from the Grameen Bank have been denounced by extremist *imams* (religious leaders) who believe the work of the Bank is opposed to the will of God in that it promotes some form of emancipation for poor women.

Censorship by force

A well-publicised example of the pressure of religious conservatism is the case of the writer Taslima Nasreen, who wrote a book criticising communal violence by Muslims against Hindus and attacking the Islamic clergy for their conservative attitudes and their oppression of women.

The storm that the book was to cause might never have happened had not Ms Nasreen given an interview to an Indian newspaper which reported her as saying that the Koran needed to be changed. She was furious and claimed she had been mischievously misquoted. The book called *Lajja* (Shame) sold over 50,000 copies after it appeared in February 1993 but was subsequently banned as offensive to Muslim conservatives.

In late 1993 a demonstration was staged in Dhaka, with many of the marchers calling for Ms Nasreen's execution. A *fatwa* or death sentence was passed by Islamic militants on her, and she had to go into hiding. The power of the extremist minority forced the government to issue charges against the writer, of offending the religious sensibilities of Muslims. Ms Nasreen came out of hiding to make a court appearance and was granted bail. While on bail she went to Sweden to receive a literary award from the Pen Guild of Swedish writers and remained in the West for a time. Having said that, if a progressive government in Dhaka invited her back and could provide protection, she would return, she is now back in Bangladesh, to take up the fight on behalf of Bangladeshi women.

Progressive critics of Ms Nasreen point out that the book has given political power to the fundamentalists, and fomented Hindu-Muslim hatred. The question that the democratic majority of the Bangladesh population must ask itself is: would Taslima Nasreen have been brought to trial if she had offended the sensibilities of Animists, Hindus or Buddhists? Is the government pandering to a minority of Muslim extremists and if so why, in a society where freedom of expression is held to be a basic human right? These are profound issues, which are still to be resolved.

Studying the Koran.

Abuse of the shalish

One of the time-honoured methods of solving community and village conflicts in Bangladesh is known as the *shalish*. This institution, which is not a court but rather a council of mediation or arbitration, derived its legitimacy from recognition by the *samaj* which in essence is the community. Its arbitrators were the elders and wise men recognised as such by the *samaj*. It was quick and efficient and did not involve poor villagers in lengthy and expensive litigation.

Unfortunately some of these *shalish* have recently been taken over by fundamentalists, who have turned them into religious courts administering the *shari'a* (Islamic religious law), which is illegal in Bangladesh. The sentences passed by these courts have been stoning, flogging, and even death.

In Sylhet in early 1993, the local *imam* found a young woman called Noorjahan guilty of adultery. She and her husband were buried waist deep in the ground and stoned, and her father and mother were given 50 lashes each. Noorjahan committed suicide shortly after the stoning. Because of public outrage the authorities acted quickly and apprehended the *imam* and seven other men. They were found guilty by the district court of bringing about the suicide of the young woman, and received nine years' imprisonment.

Other similar abuses of shalish are known to have occurred, where women have received terrible punishments for adultery. No doubt many more cases have gone unreported. If the *shalish* is to continue in its original and highly effective form the government must take action to prevent it being used by men to carry out violence against women.

21

The population issue

(far right) Jahanara Begum, a DUS-trained traditional birth attendant, on Hatiya Island, uses a visual aid to explain health care in pregnancy.

(below) Children in Bangladesh have to take a share in houshold tasks, and many work for wages; but like children anywhere, take time off to play.

Bangladesh is one of the most densely populated areas of the world; only city states like Singapore and Hong Kong have more people per square mile. Successive Bangladesh governments, under pressure mainly from multilateral agencies such as the World Bank, USAID (the US government's official aid agency), and some sections of the UN, have devised five-year plans to deal with what is perceived, mainly by non-Bangladeshis, to be the country's major problem.

Whilst most people would agree that a reduction in the rate of population growth is desirable, there is disagreement as to whether the reduction is for economic or humanitarian reasons. Those concerned with economics talk in terms of population control and reduction, and even speak of sterilisation as 'The Ultimate Solution'; while those who see

the issue from a human angle are involved in family planning and maternal and child health care. Their approach is people-centred and concerned with helping malnourished mothers, who still have to work 12 hours a day during pregnancies, have countless illnesses, and whose bodies are no longer capable of sustaining a healthy foetus.

Advocates of repressive population control programmes do not seem to understand that high infant mortality is a consequence of poverty, and poor people have many children both to replace those who die and to provide additional wage-earners for the family, and security for their old age. Falling birthrates have generally been associated with a rise in living standards, including not only higher incomes but also better medical and social security systems, and

SHAHIDUL ALAM

improvements in the standard of education, particularly for women. This has certainly been the case in the developed countries of the West; and the same demographic changes are taking place today in South Korea, Taiwan and some states in India, notably Kerala.

Forty per cent of women of child-bearing age now use contraception. But the attitude of some doctors, health workers, and even some NGOs which are involved in family planning, is a problem. Although workers are instructed to offer a range of methods, and to explain their effects, to women who come to clinics for advice, because of the low rates of literacy among poor women it is quicker and simpler to get them to sign the consent form (mandatory before any contraceptive method is prescribed) without explaining the full implications. However, other family-planning organisations put great emphasis on counselling for their clients, and organise training courses for clinic workers.

In a country like Bangladesh, many women are malnourished and suffer health problems. And some of the methods on offer are suspect to many women's organisations. Norplant, which is popular with health workers and population control agencies because it has a 'five-year life span', can sometimes produce side-effects of excessive bleeding. In one reported case, a women suffering severe bleeding insisted that the Norplant be removed from her body. Her doctor, who works for the Family Planning Association of Bangladesh, replied that he was the best judge of the matter and told the *New Nation* newspaper (24 October 1994), after 250 women took to the streets and demonstrated against Norplant, 'a woman who complains about excessive bleeding would not know if [it] is ... dangerous for her health. So if she ... asks for removal of the method the doctor will decide whether it should be removed or not.'

SHAFIQUL ALAM

The status of women

Many agencies, including those of the UN, have consistently demonstrated that there is a relationship between women's status and family size. In a recent study, the UN stated that a major precondition for further improving family planning acceptance in Bangladesh was 'giving women a stronger position, inside and outside the family, [which] will reduce the pressure on them to have children early in marriage. Increasing their level of education makes them much more confident about using contraceptive methods. In 1984-86 the total fertility rate for women with secondary or higher education was 3.3, while for women with no schooling it was 4.4. Family planning programmes cannot, however, be confined to women. Until men take more responsibility for contraception family sizes are likely to remain unnecessarily high.'

Women's place in Bengali society

Educating your daughter is like watering another man's fields.

Bengali saying

Bangladesh is a male-dominated society underpinned by Islamic tradition. Social norms and cultural restrictions confine women under the 'protection' of the men in their family. It is generally unacceptable for women to travel freely or work outside the home, and this results in a life-long economic and social dependence on men, first as a daughter, then a wife, and finally as a mother. This third stage of dependency only occurs if she is lucky enough to have a son who is prepared to assume economic responsibility for her in her old age.

Most women in Bangladesh are regarded as burdens from the day they are born. As statistics on malnutrition demonstrate, they are given less food as children. They receive the minimum of education, and statistics show that far fewer women than men are literate. They are frequently promised in marriage while still in infancy; and when married, often in their early teens, they have to take a dowry with them since they are then considered to be a 'burden' to their husband's family. Although the payment of a dowry is illegal in Bangladesh, the practice is widespread. If the dowry is regarded as insufficient or does not measure up to what was promised when the marriage was negotiated, a bride may be divorced, deserted, ill-treated or even murdered.

Women move in with their husband's extended family when they marry, and they work extremely hard processing and preparing food, carrying water, cleaning, and caring not only for their own children, but also for their husband and his relatives. It is on them that the principal burden falls of trying to ensure that sufficient food is available for their family, and often they themselves go without in order to give more food to their husband and children, particularly their sons.

Women who are left alone after being divorced, deserted, or widowed will have great difficulty in surviving if no one in their family can afford to take them in. There is very little socially acceptable employment available for women except as domestic servants. Growing poverty, and an increase in the numbers of deserted and divorced women, has resulted in more women being forced to break out of the social restrictions which surround them and search for work.

Processing and preparing food for her family takes up several hours of a woman's working day.

BADAL

Suk Jan Bibi with her
Uttaran group.

Women fight injustice

Suk Jan Bibi lives in a village near
Satkhira in south-west Bangladesh. She is
a member of group called Uttaran: 'to
overcome'. She had been married as a
child, and had a son, but then her
husband, like tens of thousands of others,
was killed in the War of Liberation. As a
young widow, Suk Jan Bibi had received
many proposals of marriage over the
years. These had been offered in
traditional fashion through marriage
brokers. Although it was a struggle to
survive as a widow with a young son,
she decided she would not remarry, and
consistently sent away the marriage
brokers with 'no' for an answer.

One evening, while bringing her goat
home from grazing, she was attacked and
raped by the son of the powerful local
landowner. Some friends found her
unconscious and carried her to the
Uttaran office, from where she was taken
to the hospital in a nearby town. The
project workers asked the doctor who
treated Suk Jan Bibi to provide them with
a certificate to state she was a rape victim.
Without this piece of paper the local
police would have taken no action. The
doctor was reluctant to do so when he
discovered the identity of the rapist.

Under intense pressure from Uttaran he
eventually gave in.

Suk Jan Bibi sought help from Uttaran
in bringing a case. Knowing that the
police would be reluctant to prosecute,
Uttaran organised a demonstration of
over 200 women to demand justice. The
accused was taken into custody but
another massive demonstration of over
1,000 men and women was necessary
before he was brought to court. These
demonstrations frightened the local
landowning families and the man was
prosecuted and jailed, but not before his
family had offered Suk Jan Bibi a large
sum of money to drop the charges. When
that failed the family tried to win her
over by promising that the rapist would
take her as his second wife if she would
withdraw the case. Suk Jan Bibi refused
the bribes and, with Uttaran, won the
day.

Uttaran had achieved victory on two
levels. They had demonstrated their
strength to the landowners and refused
to allow the rich and powerful to deprive
them of their legal rights. On a deeper
level, they had confronted and defeated
an established system of injustice against
women.

Women and development

Development agencies in Bangladesh have in the past adopted a paternalistic approach to women. Women have often been treated as beneficiaries in a 'women's project' but seldom as full participants. This can sometimes be of benefit in enabling women to realise their own strengths in a protected environment; but if women are to be enabled to develop their full potential, it will be necessary for cultural attitudes to undergo a radical change.

There is a growing feminist movement amongst educated Bangladeshi women, who are anxious to secure a better life for their 'sisters'; and many development agencies are now trying to work with such women. Advances may be slow and gradual but they are the result of what Bangladeshi women decide is desirable and possible within the context of their own lives. To help the oppressed may mean standing beside them in their own struggle, rather than prescribing the way forward for them; and will require a long-term and steadfast commitment.

A year ago, Chintabala could not even sign her name. She took an adult literacy course and now she can help her children with their homework. 'I am the first person in my family who has learnt to read and write. As parents we should encourage our children to study.'

Nurnun Nahar is a leading member of a women's group which Dwip Unnayan Sangstha (DUS), a local NGO, helped to form ten years ago. The original ten members lived in a village which was threatened by river erosion. DUS had encouraged them to begin saving, and when their village was in danger of being washed away, they were able to use their savings to buy a small piece of land elswhere on Hatiya Island.

'Saving was not easy' explained Nurnun. 'At first, we just kept back a small amount of rice from each meal, storing it and selling it. We also made some money selling poultry we had reared.' The women's group asked their husbands to contribute, but were abused and beaten up. So, when the new land was registered in the women's names, their menfolk were in no position to complain.

The group worked together to protect the land against flooding, dug a fishpond, and built houses on the plot. They make money by selling fish from their pond, and they each have a small kitchen garden which provides for some of their food needs; and they share the work of cultivating a communal field.

'We spend most of what cash we have on food,' says Nurnun. 'The second major expense is education for our children; we have to buy pencils and books for them to use at school. Otherwise, we spend the money on soap, oil, matches, and clothes.' Nurnun and the other members of her group consider themselves to be quite well-off now, compared to some of their neighbours.

'Before we got ourselves organised, we never dreamed of having our own fishpond. Now we're no longer poor; if guests come, we can catch fish from the pond to feed them. If our neighbours are in trouble, we can help them out. We couldn't do that before.

And our health is better now, because we know about using clean water to drink and wash the pots.'

DUS has provided a tubewell, and training in health and sanitation; each family has dug a pit latrine. A DUS doctor calls at the village once a month to advise the women about family planning and health care for themselves and their children. When one of the women has a baby, a DUS-trained traditional birth attendant looks after her.

The women have gained in self-confidence. 'Our husbands used to beat us all the time! Now my husband still mistreats me occasionally, but things are much better. If any of our husbands tries to hit us now, we fight back!'

Saving together

SHAFIQUL ALAM

Nurnun Nahar feeding fish in the communal pond.

The ubiquitous rickshaw

WALTER HOLT

Street scene, Dhaka. Rickshaws are a cost-effective and non-polluting form of transport, but the rickshaw wallahs earn very little for their many hours of exhausting work.

Rickshaws first made their appearance in Japan in the eighteenth century and gradually spread throughout Asia and changed from the two-wheeled vehicle with the man between the shafts to a three-wheeled bicycle-driven machine. The present rickshaw with its brightly coloured designs and motifs of folk art could be the national symbol of Bangladesh.

The rickshaw is the most important component of the transport system of Bangladesh. This human-powered machine is a very cost-effective part of the economy. Bangladesh has a bicycle manufacturing industry, and the bulk of the materials to produce the rickshaw are made locally; there are virtually no expensive imports. Roadside maintenance is cheap and provides employment for small entrepreneurs whose requirements are a space on the pavement, a set of spanners, a puncture-repair kit, and a bicycle pump. Rickshaws are very appropriate in this flat country and, in addition, they do not pollute the atmosphere. Although the government has stated that rickshaws are to be phased out, their numbers are increasing annually.

Rickshaw wallahs are exploited by *mohajans* who own fleets of 30 to 100 rickshaws which they rent on a daily two-shift basis to the wallahs. The wallah has to pull the machine for two hours to pay the rental costs before he can start making some money for himself. He is responsible for repairs, which can be frequent if the rickshaw is an old one. In the Comilla area east of Dhaka, a large number of rickshaw co-operatives have been set up. The rickshaw wallahs buy their machine from the co-operative on a hire-purchase basis and at minimum rates of interest. Should someone fall sick this is taken into consideration when repayments are due. The co-operative also has a savings system whereby members can put some of their daily earnings into a savings account.

Lutfur's story

Lutfur Rahman recognises that in one sense he is lucky. He is a rickshaw wallah under the power of a rickshaw *mohajon* but, unlike the landless agricultural labourers in the rural village from which he came, he gets work every day he is fit enough to work an eight-hour shift.

Lutfur's story is typical of many of the men pulling rickshaws around the streets of Dhaka. When he was a teenager his father lost his one acre of land to a moneylender who had the land title as collateral. Deprived of his only source of income, Lutfur's father brought his wife and six children to Dhaka to look for work. After a short time, he died, but by then young Lutfur had found work as a rickshaw wallah.

Lutfur naturally assumed financial responsibility for the entire family. He rents one room for Taka400 (£8) per month. Down the middle of the room is a cloth partition; Lutfur and his wife (a marriage his mother arranged with a girl from their home village) and two children live on one side and on the other side live his mother, his two brothers, and two sisters, with the three children of one of the sisters who is divorced.

On an average day Lutfur Rahman pulls his rickshaw 40 miles, and after he has paid the rent of the machine and the cost of minor repairs, he takes home around Taka75. He has repair bills daily since he rents an old rickshaw and the *mohajon* insists that the machine is returned in good order. As the sole breadwinner in a large extended family, he dare not argue with the *mohajon*.

Lutfur has dreamed for years of owning his own rickshaw but knows that he will never be able to afford it. A new machine is quite cheap by Western standards (about £130), but Lutfur's annual earnings are only Taka20,000 (£400). His best hope of emancipation from the *mohajon* would be to join a co-operative, but there are not many of these in his neighbourhood.

Community health care

Bangladesh, like many other Southern countries, has limited resources to spend on social services. In the absence of national community health care many NGOs are now helping poor rural and urban communities to set up their own systems.

One group of NGOs are operating successful health-care programmes which the communities themselves finance. In order to fund the services they need, families pay the equivalent of four pence per month per person into a health insurance fund. With 2,000 families enrolled, such a scheme becomes viable. The programme provides a clinic, with a doctor, and peripatetic paramedics who hold surgeries in various locations. If the paramedic cannot deal with the problem the patient will be referred to the doctor.

Fieldworkers are given training in preventive health care so that they can provide advice on health and nutrition to people involved in development projects. A tubewell has been installed to provide clean drinking water for each community.

In the longer term the communities will have a pharmacy to dispense low-cost essential drugs. A laboratory for each community is also planned, to carry out simple diagnostic tests. Both will be financed from the health insurance funds.

Essential drugs

The World Health Organisation (WHO) has long been concerned over the promotion and sale of obsolete and useless medicines in Third World countries. WHO drew up a list of 250 'essential drugs', most of which were obtainable in generic form, thus lowering the cost of medical treatment.

Bangladesh was the first country to take action, in June 1982, by banning the importation of over 1,700 locally and internationally produced drugs, which were either dangerous, or combinations of similar or incompatible ingredients, or because they could be produced by local companies instead of being imported. A list of essential drugs, in their generic forms, was drawn up for use in all sectors of the health care system. This action was met by howls of protest from the transnational drug companies, who feared a serious loss of profits if more countries followed Bangladesh's example.

Unfortunately, the new General Agreement on Tariffs and Trade liberalises international trade, and makes such 'restraints on trade' illegal, thus favouring the interests of large transnational companies. They are now free to flood the Bangladesh market with inessential pharmaceutical products.

A contributory factor to the demise of the drugs policy in Bangladesh has been the failure of the Bangladesh Medical Association (BMA) to support it. Many doctors opposed the legislation from the outset, seeing it as a threat to their professional freedom; those who own a pharmacy have a financial interest in prescribing lavishly.

Drugs for sale in a village market.

DAVE TOMSON

Photo credit: PENNY TWEEDIE

Saving lives simply

In Bangladesh the infant mortality rate is one of the highest in the world, with only eight out of ten children reaching their fifth birthday. The greatest killer of children is diarrhoea. Because of a belief that children suffering from diarrhoea should not be given food or drink, many children die who could have recovered with proper care. In fact it is vitally important to keep up the fluid intake of children suffering from diarrhoea to prevent dehydration, and withholding food will further weaken a sick child.

The Bangladesh Rural Advancement Committee (BRAC) developed an Oral Rehydration Therapy programme which they hoped would eventually reach every village in the country and drastically reduce the mortality from diarrhoea. The BRAC therapy used materials which were readily to hand in Bangladeshi homes: *gur*, a form of molasses made from sugar cane, *lobon* (salt), and water. BRAC

recruited over a thousand young women to teach mothers how to prepare the Lobon-Gur-Solution (LGS).

The women visited every household in the villages to which they were assigned and taught the 'pinch and scoop method'. At least one woman in each household was taught that a three-finger pinch of *lobon* and a scoop of *gur* in the hand, added to half-a-litre of water, would keep an infant alive while the diarrhoea was raging. The trainer also marked one container in the household at the right level for the water, and gave one-to-one instruction on caring for children with diarrhoea.

By the end of 1994 BRAC had taught the method to about 13 million households: a remarkable achievement by any standard. NGOs in other districts have followed BRAC's example, and the target set by BRAC of reaching every village must be very close indeed.

Demonstrating the 'pinch and scoop' method to a group of village women.

Disability and poverty

Disability is closely related to poverty. Many diseases which lead to impairment of mental and physical capabilities are caused by malnutrition. In a study carried out in Jamalpur district by an NGO called Social Assistance for the Rehabilitation of the Physically Vulnerable (SARPV), it was found that out of a total disabled population of between eight and nine per cent, 90 per cent of disabilities were the result of nutritional disorders: goitre, rickets, and blindness caused by vitamin A deficiency, were very common, and have displaced polio in the last two decades as the major causes of disability. Yet they are all preventable: in the case of goitre, by iodised salt; rickets by fish and plenty of sunlight; and vitamin A-deficiency blindness by green vegetables and fruit..

Spinal injuries, both paraplegic and tetraplegic, are also widespread in Bangladesh. They result from carrying head loads which are too heavy, or falling while carrying a heavy head load. Many people are injured by falling from trees when picking fruit or coconuts.

Official statistics on the incidence of disability are lacking. SARPV points out that the number of people who die from road accidents is recorded but not the number of those permanently disabled. As in the case of natural disasters, officials can always tell you how many people perished but not the numbers of those incapacitated permanently. This makes it difficult for those who are working with the disabled to address the problem effectively. SARPV and other similar organisations are putting increasing emphasis on advocacy to establish the rights of disabled people.

Shamon, who trains residents in carpentry, at the Centre for the Rehabilitation of the Paralysed.

Education and development

Bengalis have always revered their poets and philosophers and this tradition persists right down to the present day. In the past the university in Dhaka was known as the 'Cambridge of the East'; and as well as producing poets and thinkers it provided the administrative system of the Indian empire with some of its finest and ablest civil servants. It is, therefore, sad to reflect that this former excellence is in danger of disappearing because of the failure to maintain and develop the modern education systems which should sustain it.

Although primary education is free to all children, and secondary education free to girls until grade 8, not all children take advantage of this provision. Government statistics show that only 70 per cent of children enrol in primary school, of which only 10 to 15 per cent are girls; and 27 per cent of children enrol for secondary education. Only 25 per cent of those enrolling finish five years of basic education and of these, over 90 per cent are boys from middle-class homes.

A clear measure of the success of the education system in any country is the general level of literacy. In Bangladesh only around 32 per cent of the population are literate, the majority of whom are middle-class males. The low figure is related to the high rate of drop-out from primary school.

Literacy is the key to so many other aspects of a nation's development programme. This is summed up by the Bangladesh Rural Advancement Committee (BRAC):

Effective development is dependent on human development and human development in its turn is dependent on education. Broad-based literacy has been one of the most important enabling factors in the economic success of newly developing countries. Improvements in health and reduction in birth rates also depend on literacy, particularly among women. In Bangladesh over a million workers enter the country's labour market annually... Jobs can be created only if there is a skilled work-force. Basic literacy provides the floor for skill development.

If Bangladesh is to share in the rapid economic development that has characterised other parts of Asia, a determined effort must be made to improve educational standards. The Asian countries which have developed most efficiently and quickly over the last two decades, such as Taiwan, South Korea, and Malaysia, have literacy rates comparable with, and even better than, some countries in the North. The new

SHAFIQUL ALAM

Lakhi is reading an article she wrote in a magazine about her life as a tribal woman. She never went to school as a child, but took an adult literacy course run by a local NGO.

profitable industries of electronics, computers, and communications require a work force that can be trained to use high-tech equipment. People must be able to read and write before such training can take place.

The reluctance of the international business community to invest in Bangladesh is undoubtedly related to the extremely low rates of literacy and educational achievement.

A school in a slum

Notun Bazaar is a *bustee* (slum) area of the large town of Khulna in south-west Bangladesh. It has a population of around 16,000 people who live in appalling conditions in one-roomed dwellings made of mud, rushes; and cardboard boxes. There is no water or electricity supply and the area is flooded incessantly in the monsoon season.

Notun Bazaar has developed as a result of rural-urban migration. Many of the people who live there lost their land to village moneylenders to whom they were trapped in debt. Others had become unemployed because of changes in the rural economy. To have stayed in the villages where they were born would have condemned them to the inevitable hunger and misery that are the consequences of landlessness and unemployment. At least in the city there was a chance of earning enough to stay alive, even though living conditions were terrible. These families live in the Notun Bazaar because they have no option; there is nowhere else for them to go.

Yet in the midst of all this squalor and deprivation there exists a small school which bears the wonderful name of Anand Niketan – the 'House of Joy'.

Anand Niketan was started in 1987 by the *bustee* dwellers with support from an NGO called Gono Shahajjo Sangstha. At first, it occupied three rooms in a building which the *bustee* people constructed from bamboo and rush matting. About 200 children attended Primaries One, Two, and Three in a two-

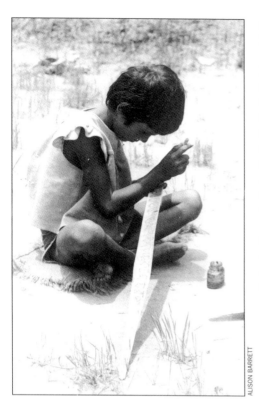

ALISON BARRETT

shift system and were taught by part-time teachers.

By 1991 a brick building had been built, with six rooms, desks, blackboards, and other teaching equipment. The enrolment had increased to 487 children and young adults spread over five classes. They are being taught by six full-time and five part-time teachers. There are now three shifts daily, and young adults who work in the nearby fish factory are also attending Anand Niketan when they can.

Anand Niketan is a lively and well-attended school and shows that people can overcome the most difficult circumstances and make real advances through their own efforts.

(above far left) **Children on their way to school in the bustee.**
(below far left) **Haroon Begum, one of the teachers at the school.**

(left) **Using a palm-leaf stalk to practise writing.**
(below) **Children at Bhognagar Primary School enjoy performing songs and dances.**

SHAFIQUL ALAM

Devising a relevant curriculum

When planning a new educational initiative, BRAC realised the importance of understanding the reasons for the high drop-out rate. Motivation to send children to school is poor when the parents themselves are illiterate. Curricula are frequently inappropriate, especially in rural areas, and the cost of providing clothing and educational materials is too great for most poor families. But by far the most compelling reason why large numbers of Bangladeshi children do not attend school is because they are needed to work on the family plot or to go out to earn money. BRAC devised a curriculum and timetable which took account of this: the Non-Formal Primary Education (NFPE) programme.

The NFPE programme recognised that schooling must be organised around work demands on children's time. Only two to three hours a day are spent in school, at times which have been decided in consultation with the families concerned. The schools are closed during seasons of intensive agricultural work, such as planting or harvesting. As well as acquiring the basic skills in reading, writing, and arithmetic, the children are given lessons in health, hygiene, nutrition and community studies, related to everyday life in the village.

Absenteeism is chronic among teachers in the state system, so BRAC takes great care in the recruitment of teachers. Criteria for selection are strict and the person selected must teach in the village where he or she lives. BRAC prefers teachers to be married, and hopes to reach a target of 70 per cent of teachers in its schools being women. BRAC trains its own teachers in regional centres and runs refresher courses for all teachers in the areas where they work. Teachers are supervised on a regular basis by experienced educational advisers.

One of the objectives of the programme is to achieve universal primary education in Bangladesh by the year 2000. In a meeting with the Education Minister of Lesotho in December 1994, BRAC staff said they had opened over 25,000 NFPE schools which 800,000 children attended. The Minister was in Bangladesh to study the NFPE programme which he hoped could be adapted to the needs of Lesotho's children. BRAC is also transferring its NFPE methodology to Uganda, Somalia, Burundi, Tanzania, Zambia and Namibia.

Many Bangladeshi children do not attend school because their labour is needed by the family.

RAQU

An evaluation of the programme by the World Bank reported:

The unit cost of the programme is around Taka500, which is higher than the unit cost of formal primary education (around Taka200). But if the wastage factor in the formal system is considered [the NFPE] programme stands out as much more cost-effective and affordable by a poor developing country like Bangladesh.

Literacy for a purpose

Friends in Village Development Bangladesh (FIVDB), situated in a rural area in the extreme north-east of the country, has developed a functional literacy programme which is so successful that it is now used widely throughout Bangladesh.

FIVDB concentrates on the 'functional' aspect, making sure that literacy is relevant to the needs of the people taking the intensive three-month courses. Numeracy is taught using calculations which would be necessary in the market,

the home, or for running a small rural business such as duck raising or goat breeding. Literacy teachers use material which features agriculture, civil and legal rights, and community issues. FIVDB works with the most disadvantaged groups so that they can 'improve and control their own situation through cooperation, self-help and self-reliance'.

By 1994, over 5,000 students had completed the functional literacy programme and the operation was expanding. In keeping with FIVDB's objective of reaching the most disadvantaged, many of the courses are exclusively for women. About 95 per cent of the students have had no previous schooling whatsoever. Khodeza is proof of the success of the scheme. She is the teacher of a class of 20 women at Bhawaltila. She herself was illiterate a year ago but is now handling the materials and classes with complete confidence.

Women in a literacy class in a resettlement camp outside Dhaka. Former pavement dwellers, they were moved to the camp as part of a government slum-clearance programme.

Water: a blessing or a curse

SHAHIDUL ALAM

(above) Enjoying water from a newly-installed tube-well.

(below) Post-cyclone 1991. High tide at Shrujodia village, Nijhum Dwip.

Bangladesh has always experienced some degree of flooding since it first formed from the rich alluvial soil washed down from the Great Himalaya. Flooding is a fact of life to the people of Bangladesh and they demonstrate great resilience and skill in coping with it. The familiar images of women wading through four feet of flood water to fetch clean drinking water may evoke pity; but such images also show the strength and resourcefulness of people who are getting on with their lives, in difficult circumstances.

The two major crops grown in Bangladesh, rice for internal markets and jute, of which 90 per cent is for export, can truly be termed aquatic plants. The great rivers which flow into Bangladesh provide abundant water for growing rice

SHAHIDUL ALAM

and jute, and monsoon flooding, which normally affects about one third of the country, is regarded by farmers as beneficial. They have developed agricultural practices to make use of the floodwater for their crops. It is when flooding increases beyond the normal level that it causes problems.

After the devastating floods which occurred in 1987 and 1988, extensive studies have been carried out of flooding and flood control in Bangladesh. Deforestation in the Himalayas has been blamed for increased run-off from the mountains and although this may be significant locally, other experts question whether the effects would be felt far downstream. Some studies blame increased flooding on heavy siltation blocking the natural drainage system. Other consultants claim that there is no underlying trend towards increased flooding and that the major floods of the past few years have simply been statistical extremes. One thing is certain: the causes of flooding in Bangladesh are many and complex.

There are divergent views as to how the problem of flooding should be tackled. Some experts favour permanent embankments to be built at enormous expense to contain the rivers, others opt for allowing the rivers to overflow their banks but developing better early-warning systems and building flood refuges in the villages.

What is vital is that the human dimension, not always taken into account by large donors, is at the forefront of the debate. The government of Bangladesh has stated that any flood control plans must 'encourage popular support by involving beneficiaries in the planning, design and operation'. Solutions which threaten to displace the poor, increase landlessness, and destroy rural communities must be firmly rejected.

The politics of water

A water-sharing agreement was made between Bangladesh and India in 1985. A persistent cause of controversy is the

(above) **Floods are something people in Bangladesh have learned to live with.**

Farakka Barrage, which India built on the Ganges just outside the border with Bangladesh. It was designed to regulate the amount of water in the Hoogly river, which flows out of the Ganges and south through West Bengal to Calcutta. However, data show that the amount of water going down the Hoogly in regular flood has been reduced from 130,000 to 80,000 cusecs. (A cusec is the flow of water in cubic feet per second.) The Bangladesh government claims the extra 50,000 cusecs are being diverted into Bangladesh, adding to their problem.

(below) **Water everywhere, but only water from the pump is fit to drink.**

The Farakka Barrage can also be used to prevent water going down the Ganges into Bangladesh during the dry season. In late 1994 the north-west of Bangladesh was facing a serious drought and the government claimed the amount of water being allowed into the system by Farakka was only 25 per cent of normal, the flow having been reduced from about 40,000 to 10,000 cusecs. This has meant that the aquifers in the region are not recharging, and if the rainfall is very light, the situation becomes extremely serious. Farakka is also causing problems in the south-west as salinity comes further and further up the river system, with far less fresh water coming down via the Ganges.

Working on strengthening an embankment, part of a community-based flood-prevention project.

CLARE HANTON KHAN

There is also major disagreement on how to control and use the Brahmaputra. India wants to build reservoirs in its north-eastern state of Assam with a canal through Bangladesh to carry water to the Ganges during the dry season. Bangladesh agrees on the need for reservoirs but wants them to be in Nepal on tributaries of the major rivers, presumably so that India will not have total control of the water.

The course of the Brahmaputra illustrates the need for regional agreements on water use. From its source in the Chemayungdung Mountains, which are partly in Nepal, it flows through Tibet as the Yarlung Yangbo and goes through Lhasa on its way to China where it becomes simply the Yangbo. At the Chinese town of Pei, where the largest hydroelectric complex in the world is planned, it turns south and enters the north-eastern Indian state of Arunachal Pradesh, where it is called the Dihang. It then meanders through Assam, where it acquires the name Brahmaputra, and enters Bangladesh near the northern town of Kurigram. In Bangladesh its name changes again to the Jamuna, which it keeps until it joins the Ganges and eventually ends up in the Bay of Bengal.

The Flood Action Plan

The Flood Action Plan is a project supported heavily by the World Bank, Asian Development Bank, United Nations Development Programme (UNDP), and almost every other Western bilateral donor. But the project has been criticised by local activists and international agencies on environmental and humanitarian grounds.

Extensive studies, costing a great deal of money, have been carried out to analyse the problem of flooding. As a result, Bangladesh now has a comprehensive and highly sophisticated data base on its rivers, water systems, and weather patterns. Programmes are being developed to increase awareness of floods and give early warning of danger so that people can protect themselves and their possessions.

The ultimate aim of the Plan is to exert some degree of control over the major rivers. However, environmentalists argue that the rivers are not yet settled enough for control by 'permanent' engineering, and move continuously, sometimes with devastating results. Groynes and embankments constructed over the last two decades are either now in middle of major rivers or are damaged beyond repair. Many sluice gates are so silted up that they cannot be opened or closed. And these great rivers still move. The Brahmaputra has moved nearly fifty miles westward in the last hundred years. Together with the rivers Ganges, Kosi and Teesta, this changing hydrological pattern presents an immense control problem.

Different priorities

Ecologists and nutritionists have also condemned the FAP since it interferes with food chains and agricultural and fisheries systems. Fish migrate on and off the floodplain to breed and feed, and provide a valuable source of protein for peasant families. Farmers also need the floodwaters for growing rice and jute, and the silt deposited, which is rich in minerals, makes the soil fertile. People who live beside the major rivers have been dealing with floods for thousands of years. Families living on the *chars* (islands) in the middle of the great rivers will either move on to raised earthen platforms or use the roof of the house and a *bhela* (raft made of banana trees) until the floodwaters recede.

Studies carried out by the author with communities living near the

Floods are a familiar part of life for this young Bangladeshi artist.

RUTH VERSFELD

People took refuge in this newly-constructed cyclone refuge during the cyclone in 1991.

Brahmaputra showed that, while people wanted flood protection and were prepared to contribute to its cost, they had other, more urgent priorities. When people were asked to rank their needs, flood protection generally came fourth or fifth. Of far greater importance in all communities were better health care, the provision of education for children, local job opportunities for the landless, and better credit facilities at local banks for farmers and fishermen.

The effect of some flood control systems has been to deprive people of a valuable community resource. By creating enclosed and controlled water systems where formerly there were natural wetlands, great areas of common fishing grounds have been denied to poor people. These waters have been taken over by rich landowners who either market the fish locally for profit or create shrimp farms and export the product to Northern markets.

Targeting vulnerability

Even in a disaster, there is potential for development. The process known as the Integrated Disaster Preparedness and Development Project (IDPDP) starts by assessing the vulnerability of a community to disasters. The involves the participation of the entire community, meeting together with NGO staff to analyse the problems they face. When it becomes clear that the community suffers a high level of vulnerability, a plan of action is devised which integrates a development component with disaster preparedness.

One such project is being implemented on a *char* in the Brahmaputra River. A char is a low-lying island which can be farmed by poor families on a seasonal basis. The community of Manab Mukti, which has about 5,000 households, lives on one of these *chars* which is two hours' boat ride from the district town of Sirajganj on the right bank of the

Brahmaputra. To help them to cope with the regular flooding of the Brahmaputra they were trained in disaster preparedness, helped to raise their homesteads above regular flood levels, and make a platform on which to keep their livestock; to build a latrine; and to instal extra piping to raise the community tubewells above the flood levels and ensure that clean drinking water is available during the floods. Community members were taught how to connect the modified tubewell and how to maintain it with a tool set provided by the project. To enable people to survive extreme floods, two community shelters were built which also had tubewells and latrines.

Further disaster-preparedness measures were linked directly to development goals. A boat was provided for use in emergencies to take people to the mainland, to bring food to the char or to obtain medical attention when accidents or serious illnesses occurred. At other times, the boat could be used as a ferry, to generate income for the community. Out of the normal community savings account an emergency fund was started, to be drawn on when floods occurred.

The community provided labour and materials to build the various structures necessary for flood preparedness, and planted flood-resistant trees and shrubs around the *char* to compact the soil and to act as a natural barrier to the water.

Alongside these activities to prepare for emergencies, came the development components of strengthening the local institutions and training community workers. Functional education was also provided, together with a credit scheme, which would enable families to take loans for agricultural purposes, especially to grow flood-resistant crops. Loans could also be provided for economic activities which the floods could not easily disrupt.

Manab Mukti is now a strong and flourishing community. Its experience shows how vulnerability analysis, carried out in a participative way, can lead to development initiatives which ultimately reduce that vulnerability.

The threat of global warming

Because so much of Bangladesh lies at or close to sea level, it is one of the countries most vulnerable to any rise in sea level caused by global warming. Even a small rise in level in the Bay of Bengal would have a devastating effect in Bangladesh. Predictions of climatic changes vary, but many climatologists warn of a significant rise in temperature within the next fifty years. While countries like Holland, also at risk, may be able to afford the many billions of pounds necessary to extend their sea-defences, Bangladesh has little hope of doing so, and the long-term future prospects of increased flooding and eventual abandonment of large areas of the country, with huge numbers of people displaced as a consequence, are grim indeed.

Foreign aid: development and dependency

In the 1980s Bangladesh had become highly dependent on foreign funding for large new projects, such as power stations, bridges and roads, and for major items of its domestic budget, including the importing of raw materials and spare parts.

But despite steady increases from year to year in external aid, the poor were getting poorer. Between 1985 and 1987 per capita income actually dropped from $135 to $128; life expectancy remained constant at 48 years; infant mortality remained at a high level of around 130 deaths per 1,000 live births; and landlessness increased annually.

The billions of dollars in aid poured into Bangladesh had little effect on poverty because most of it was spent on heavily capitalised infrastructure projects. These may have some indirect effect on the lives of poor people, but what people really want is better health and education services, better village roads rather than motorways, and credit facilities to help them to improve agriculture and raise their incomes. Most big Western donors found these small-scale projects too difficult to measure and administer.

The degree of dependence by Bangladesh on aid had political conse-quences. Rehman Sobhan, a Bangladeshi economist, alleged that aid donors behaved as if their 'generosity' gave them the right to intervene in the running of the country; they attempted to influence government policy on a wide range of issues. Development should be a process whereby aid becomes less necessary as people's lives improve through the mobilisation of their own resources and the natural resources of the country. In Bangladesh the reverse was happening.

In the last few years, Bangladesh's dependency on aid has diminished. Investment is still sluggish, but with a respectable balance of payments, low inflation (around 4 per cent), recent stable commodity prices, and a domestic budget entirely financed by local resources, Bangladesh is moving in the right direction. By financing more and more of its own development and investment, it will be able to break free of the political strings attached to foreign aid.

Britain's bilateral aid

In 1993-94 the Overseas Development Administration (ODA) spent £55m in Bangladesh on behalf of the British taxpayer. Most of this, around £45m, was in the form of project aid, of which half went to government infrastructure programmes of gas and electricity schemes and bridges. The remainder went on human development projects in the fields of health and population, education, and women in development, and was channelled through both the NGO and the formal sector.

A further £5m was spent on training Bangladesh professionals: between four and five hundred people. Most of them went to British institutions, but some went to other countries in the region where the training was more appropriate (for example, courses on fisheries development in the Asian Institute of Technology in Bangkok). In future, training will be increasingly sought in institutes in the region.

ODA is placing more emphasis on assessment and monitoring of projects. The Aid Management Office Dhaka (AMOD) has been set up, headed by a senior ODA official who manages and coordinates the work of specialist consultants in a number of fields including fisheries, agriculture, health and population, education, and engineering. An economist and a social development specialist are also part of AMOD, to analyse the economic viability of projects and determine the social and economic impacts.

A further change has been to increase funding to Bangladeshi NGOs. Proshika, an NGO working in both rural and urban areas, is to receive approximately £10m; BRAC has received considerable funds for rural development, especially its work on women's health and in non-formal primary education; and the AMOD is looking at ways of providing funding to smaller NGOs. The AMOD is discussing with the Grameen Bank some new initiatives for training and advice to farmers on fish farming.

These positive changes have come about largely as a result of dialogue with NGOs and advocacy groups, which in the past have been critical of the way in which bilateral aid was used.

Multilateral funding

In 1992 funding from multilateral sources amounted to 53 per cent of the total aid disbursed to Bangladesh, which was roughly £1.25bn. Over £500m was in the form of loans mainly from the World Bank (WB) and the Asian Development Bank (ADB). In late 1994 the ADB committed a further £800m to be spent over a four-year period. These loans may be 'soft' in that the interest charged is lower than that of commercial banks, but they still have to be repaid; and they are dependent on the introduction of stringent economic measures. The banks insist on liberalisation of markets and deregulation of the economy before a loan is agreed. These conditionalities may have serious effects on poor people.

Finance minister Saifur Rahman claimed that some aspects of conditionality created social problems for his government. He cited as an example the demand that the jute industry be restructured. This meant laying off thousands of workers, which resulted in strikes and protests by men who faced unemployment and poverty, after years of working in the industry.

While market forces can play a powerful role in stimulating economic growth, structural adjustment policies must be balanced with a concern for equity, and protection of the basic rights of the poor. The current World Bank policy of deregulating labour markets will merely increase 'poverty in employment', as wages fall; and there is little evidence to suggest that it will actually lead to economic growth.

Another unintentional effect of large amounts of bilateral and multilateral aid is the widespread corruption which it can create. The effects seem to leave no one untouched; contractors, consultants, bureaucrats, and politicians all have much to gain personally from the flow of aid. The control of aid projects gives immense power to politicians and bureaucrats, and fortunes can be made by suppliers and contractors. The power and patronage reach right down to deciding who gets the job of breaking the stones in the construction of rural roads. The result is an ever widening gap between the minority elite and the impoverished 95 per cent of the population. The flow of aid may be adding to the problem of gross inequalities in Bangladesh society.

A future for jute?

Bangladesh, when it was East Bengal in the days of the British Raj, was a colony devoted to the production of a single export crop: jute. The high rainfall and humid climate were perfect for growing this fibrous crop, for which there was a steady demand for use in the carpet and sacking industries, and later for the manufacture of linoleum. It deserved its name of 'the golden fibre'. Yet the contribution jute made to the economy was less than it might have been, because all the manufacturing processes, which add value to the raw material, were carried out in Britain. The town of Dundee in Scotland became the 'jute capital' of the world.

In the twentieth century the discovery of synthetic fibres such as polyethylene virtually destroyed the jute industry. Between 1970 and 1982 about 200,000 hectares of the Bangladesh countryside were taken out of jute production. Although Bangladesh still accounts for over 70 per cent of world production, farmers are reluctant to grow a crop when they are not guaranteed a good price for it.

Recently, new methods have been developed of reducing green jute to a pulp which can be made into paper. In Sylhet in late 1994 a local newspaper started to use paper produced from jute. Other smaller projects have used jute to

Ropes in all shapes and sizes for sale in a village market. The use of nylon ropes is increasing, even in a country which is the world's major jute producer.

SHAHIDUL ALAM

produce high quality stationery and greeting cards. South Korea has expressed an interest in funding a joint venture which would export jute pulp, and India has suggested it might import jute pulp for its paper industry. There are already four large pulp mills in Bangladesh and the government is exploring the possibility of buying jute directly from farmers.

In a village some 30 miles from Dhaka, seven women, with the technical assistance of the Intermediate Technology Development Group and economic assistance from a local NGO called the Socio-Economic Development Society, have set up a small factory. They produce handmade stationery and cards, and control the entire process, from the chemical preparation of the jute fibre, through machining the fibre into pulp, and eventually putting block-printed designs on the finished products.

Using jute in paper production on a large scale could reduce the number of trees which have to be cut down. At a time when international concern for the environment is becoming a powerful force, jute as a biodegradable and readily renewable resource may once again become the golden fibre.

The Jute Works

After the War of Liberation, thousands of women were left destitute. Their fathers or husbands had been killed in the war and they had no way of earning a living to support themselves. In an attempt to help some of these women, a local organisation, now known as the Jute Works, was set up to train women in craftwork using jute.

From modest beginnings the Jute Works has expanded enormously and is now a large, financially self-sufficient, totally Bangladeshi organisation, which sells its products all over the world. In Europe, Oxfam Trading is a good customer, and in 1993 bought over seven per cent of the total production of the Jute Works. This was worth about £90,000 and included the sikas, mats, and bags which

Soaking jute to remove the soft outer layers of the stalks.

are a familiar sight in Oxfam shop windows. In 1993 the Jute Works exported about £1.25m worth of goods, which were produced by over 6,500 women working from their homes and getting a fair reward for their skills.

But the Jute Works is more than just a marketing organisation. It encourages the women who work for it to form self-help savings groups, and also runs a provident security fund for individual women in need. Through the savings groups, women are able to buy chickens or a goat and further increase their income.

Earnings from handicrafts alone can never provide an economic solution to a poor woman's problems, nor does part-time work carried out at home really challenge the conventions of a society which denies a full economic and social role to most women. However, by providing an opportunity for women to meet together for education and awareness-raising, the Jute works is making a more significant contribution to women's lives than merely providing a source of supplementary income.

NICK FOGDEN

(above) **Craftswoman working at home.**

(below) **Testing new product designs in the Jute Factory workshop.**

LIZ CLAYTON

Exports, ecology, and economy

In 1991 British imports of shrimps from Bangladesh were worth £10m. In the financial year 1990-91 fish products, totalling £125m, of which shrimps are the most lucrative, represented over eight per cent of Bangladesh's total exports. They were only exceeded by garments and jute manufactured goods. Shrimp processing plants can get up to five years' exemption from income tax, which illustrates the importance the government places on shrimp exports as a source of foreign exchange.

The shrimp industry, which 20 years ago barely existed, has grown at a phenomenal rate. It was wealthy entrepreneurs who recognised the potential in shrimp cultivation for export and started buying up or leasing land from peasant farmers in the flood plains around the Bay of Bengal. But there are many questionable aspects of this industry.

The shrimp ponds in the coastal plains are constructed on land which was formerly used for rice. Peasant farmers who have leased their land claim that the increase in salinity required for shrimp cultivation has reduced rice yields from one and three quarter tons to around half a ton per acre. It could take many years to restore the fertility of land which has been flooded with brackish water for the shrimps.

Small stock-pond where shrimp fry are kept until large enough to be released into the big shrimp-pond beyond.

SHAHIDUL ALAM

Large profits are made from shrimp production yet it is almost impossible to find out how they are divided between producers, processors, shippers, and marketing organisations. A group of small cultivators, who took their land back from an entrepreneur and formed a co-operative to grow shrimps, expected to make about £350 clear profit per acre. However, working backwards from the price of shrimps sold in British markets, the total cash value should be in excess of £2,000 per acre. Even after marketing and transport costs have been allowed for, it is clear that small producers are not getting a fair share of the profits.

Shrimp farming has increased unemployment among the rural poor, since it is a capital intensive operation requiring little labour input. Many landless labourers and their families have been forced to leave the area to look for work in the city of Khulna. It is ironic that the women from the Khulna slums, whose husbands previously found work on land now given over to shrimp ponds, are now being employed cleaning shrimps in the city in terrible working

Casting a net for shrimps.

conditions for an average wage of only £7 per month.

Bangladesh, which has some of the severest nutritional problems in the world, is exporting protein in the form of a luxury product for the rich Northern consumer. In the past, shrimps were a valuable part of the diet of poor people in coastal areas, but they are now becoming very scarce because the fry are being collected to stock the shrimp ponds.

These are just some of the problems and contradictions inherent in this particular method of earning foreign exchange. While there is a great need to develop profitable exports, shrimp cultivation is of questionable benefit to the people of Bangladesh.

Stealing to survive

Mohammed Hassan lives with his wife and six children in the village of Agerhat in the South Khulna coastal plain. He is a landless labourer who lost his inherited one-acre plot over five years ago. He had borrowed money to plant a crop of rice which failed when a cyclone struck the district. Having put up his small piece of

BADAL

land as collateral for the loan, the moneylender claimed it.

Hassan made ends meet by getting seasonal agricultural work near his village. It was difficult but with a winter rice crop and a wet season jute cycle he and his family could just survive, until a wealthy man from Dhaka bought out all the small cultivators and flooded the area with saline water to create the right conditions for shrimp production. Hassan's main source of income had disappeared.

Hassan and many like him were faced with some hard decisions. One option was to move to Khulna in the hope that he could find some casual work in the jute mills or perhaps in the docks. Since he owned a small house in Agerhat village and knew that living conditions in Khulna would be very much worse, he decided to stay put and find some other way to earn money.

Hassan is now one of a small group of villagers who steal shrimps from the ponds of the large cultivators. Working at night he and his fellows select a pond and take shrimps from it, using a small net. It is a dangerous business since the landlords maintain a well-armed private militia.

This activity has become almost legitimised. Agents visit the villages and ask no questions about the origins of the shrimps they buy. The shrimps are then sold on to processing plants in Khulna and, again, the owners of these factories ask no questions. No doubt Hassan and his friends receive well below the market rate for their dangerous and illegal work, but it is the only way to survive.

(above) Immature shrimp. It will grow another two inches before it is ready for the export market.

(below) Bamboo bridge across a shrimp-pond.

Ethnic minorities

Bangladesh, in common with every country in Asia, has citizens from minority ethnic groups whose cultures and customs do not fit easily with those of the majority. Although they make up less than one per cent of the population, they are very diverse, with 17 distinct ethnic groups living in the Chittagong Hill Tracts area and three others in Sylhet, Mymensingh, and Rajshahi. None of them are Muslim. Some are Buddhists, Hindus, or Animists; others, such as the Garos of Mymensingh, have been converted to Christianity by a variety of different sects.

The major issue which has threatened their existence has been rights to land.

For a good many years, Bangladeshis from the plains have been moving, voluntarily with government backing in some cases, and in others involuntarily because of pressure on land, into the homelands of the minorities. Relations between lowland settlers and minority groups had been fairly harmonious in the past, but in the 1980s more than 25,000 lowland farmers migrated into the hill areas, especially around Chittagong, and serious conflicts occurred.

Large-scale development programmes have also disrupted the lives of indigenous people. In 1963 the Pakistan government built a dam with US help at Kaptai in the Chittagong Hills which

Inside a house in the Chittagong Hills. The people who live here have their own distinctive culture and way of life.

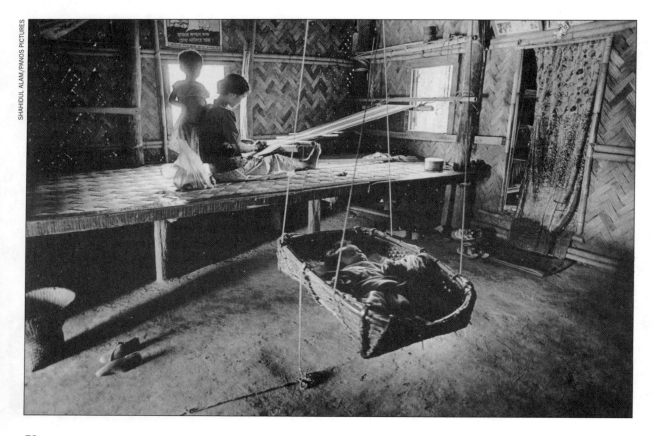

SHAHIDUL ALAM/PANOS PICTURES

displaced 100,000 people; one group, the Chakmas, was particularly badly affected. More recently, illegal and legal logging, and oil exploration, brought further deterioration to the environment. A guerrilla war started between the Shanti Bahini (Tribal Army of Freedom) and the Bangladesh military. Amnesty International claimed that thousands of hill people were killed by the Bangladesh army. Large numbers of Chakmas left the area and settled in the neighbouring Indian state of Tripura.

In November 1993 a violent incident at a place called Naniarchar in the Chittagong Hill Tracts area resulted in deaths and injuries. It began when the army fired blank shots to break up a demonstration by students from ethnic minorities. Bangladeshi settlers in the area joined in the ensuing battle, burning houses and shops and attacking people from ethnic minorities.

After a commission of enquiry the Prime Minister promised that 'the government will do everything possible to protect the tribal identity. There is neither enmity and difference nor cultural conflicts among the members of different communities. We live here as Bangladeshis.' (*Dhaka Courier* 31 December 1993). The Chakmas (who make up the great majority of the Shanti Bahini) agreed to return to their homelands from India. It remains to be seen whether the government of Khaleda Zia can protect their rights to their ancestral land and maintain peace in the area.

Shopkeeper and his wife in the village of Chimbuk, Chittagong Hills.

53

Communal violence

Ancient Hindu temple, Dhaka.

Community conflict based on religious and ethnic differences has long been a part of South Asian societies. Tension has been felt to varying degrees since Muslims and Hindus have lived together, but recent events in India have had alarming consequences in Bangladesh.

When Hindu fundamentalists claimed the Babri Mosque site in Ayodhaya was the location of the birth place of Ram (God) it set Indian Hindus against Indian Muslims in an orgy of killing and looting. In Bangladesh, Muslim fundamentalists attacked Hindus, especially in Chittagong, burning their homes and temples and looting their possessions. No one was brought to trial for these criminal acts.

According to civil rights activists in Bangladesh, this has created a permanent climate of fear for all minority groups. The Coordinating Council for Human Rights in Bangladesh (CCHRB) stated: 'The inactivity of the administration, the members of the police, and other law enforcing agencies and also the Government, to prevent such communal atrocities have encouraged the idea that the Government and its agencies have a tacit support for the persecution of religious minorities.'

CCHRB has catalogued a list of attacks by Muslims against Hindus throughout the country. These included threats to the lives of Hindus and in some cases other minorities. Durga Puja, a major Hindu festival, was a solemn affair in 1993, with participants wearing black armbands and flying black flags to draw attention to the plight of Hindus. The government, according to the organisers, tried to persuade them to mark the festival as usual with gaiety and songs and dances but they refused.

In the current atmosphere of fear and distrust, thousands of Hindu families are migrating to West Bengal. To halt this exodus the government has issued new bank regulations, which prevent individuals from religious minorities withdrawing large sums of money. But unless the government can guarantee that the human rights of all Bangladeshis, of whatever religious or ethnic identity, will be equally respected, communal violence between different groups will remain a constant threat, and will present a further barrier to the nation's economic and social development.

The garment industry

The garment industry in Bangladesh represents something of an economic miracle. Whereas there were only nine clothing factories in 1977, there are now more than 1,500. The value of exports of finished garments increased from around £150,000 in 1980 to a staggering £815m in 1993, making it by far the largest export industry in Bangladesh.

Data provided by the Bangladesh Garment Exporters and Manufacturers Association (BGMEA) show that the US is the biggest customer, taking over half of all garments produced. UK imports in 1992 were worth around £45m.

For the decade 1981-91 the employment statistics are also phenomenal. The total number of employees rose from 4,500 in 1981 to 789,000 a decade later. Although women make up just over 80 per cent of the total workforce, they are mostly in lower-paid jobs.

Unfortunately, because Bangladesh has to import almost all the raw materials and machinery to manufacture the garments, the economic value added to the products is limited. If Bangladesh were to produce sufficient cotton, and make the machinery necessary for the industry, the profits would be much greater. The industry is also hampered by the restrictive quotas imposed by industrialised countries in the North on products made by poor Southern countries, in order to protect their own manufactures.

But the success of the garment industry demonstrates that there are entrepreneurs and workers, especially women, in Bangladesh whose skill and hard work can make a huge impact on industrial development if given the opportunity to do so.

WALTER HOLT

Workers in a textile factory, Dhaka. Almost all the operatives are women; the supervisors are men.

These women have been trained and provided with sewing machines by a local NGO, and can make money by working in their own homes.

Gender issues in the garment industry

It has been argued that the growth of the Bangladesh garment industry has done more to change the situation of women in a few years than NGOs have done in the last 20. A large number of young women have been given a degree of economic emancipation that never before seemed possible in the slums of the cities where most of them live, or in the rural villages that many of them left to escape poverty. But a price has had to be paid for this social change.

The conditions in which they work are appalling. The machinery is frequently dangerous, the rooms are overcrowded, and the respect for health and safety standards is non-existent. When the authorities attempt to enforce the Factory Act they are told that the manufacturers will not meet their export targets if the Act is observed too strictly. The wages are low: £15 a month is the average wage, and if there are no orders workers are laid-off temporarily. Despite these drawbacks, women factory-workers can now make choices which previously did not exist.

These young women can delay marriage if they wish, even though they are an attractive marriage prospect to young men who have no jobs and want to live off their earnings. If their families attempt to force a husband on them they can refuse, because they now contribute significantly to the family economy. If they were still living in a village, they would have been married at 14 or 15 and had two children by the time they were 20.

The other price that has had to be paid is the erosion of labour rights in the factories. Trade unionism is discouraged; when women join the union they risk being sacked, because there are at least five others waiting for every job.

Child labour

BADAL

This boy is a skilled
weaver, and works
for many hours a day
at his carpet loom.
His wages make a
vital contribution to
his family's budget.

Child labour, especially the employment of young girls in menial and domestic service, has always been a feature of the economies of the South Asian region, and Bangladesh is no exception. Thousands of village children have traditionally been brought into towns by the urban rich and middle classes to be domestic servants. These children were frequently only given food and a charpoy to sleep on as payment for long hours scrubbing floors and washing clothes.

In recent years, with the expansion of the garment industry, many girl children are now employed in clothing factories, working long hours but at least receiving some wages. Conservative estimates in Bangladesh put the number of factory girls of 16 years and below at somewhere between 30 and 35 per cent, and children under 14 years at around 12 per cent. These young workers have attracted the attention of both international and national humanitarian organisations concerned with the plight of children. The Factory Act of 1965, enacted in the Pakistan period, seeks to control the use of child labour in factories, but it has never been observed.

There are moves in the US to ban the import of any products made by children under the age of 15. This could mean that 100,000 young Bangladeshis in the garment industry could be thrown onto the streets. These children will be hard put to survive since the majority of them have no security whatsoever other than their current employment in the garment industry.

Under pressure from international agencies the Bangladesh Garment Manufacturers and Exporters Association (BGMEA) agreed to lay off between 8,000 and 10,000 young workers. These children took to the streets and demonstrated, claiming that the alternatives to employment in the garment industry were a life on the streets or prostitution. The decision to sack them was rescinded but the BGMEA said it would stop recruiting girls under 14. It also conceded that those already employed between the ages of 12 to 14 years would only do light work.

Local NGOs such as Gono Shahajja Sangstha (GSS) argue that child labour in a country like Bangladesh needs to be looked at in the context of the alternatives for these children. In a meeting with the BGMEA a new regime for girls under 14 years was agreed, under which GSS would provide schooling for them for two hours each day and they would work for a further six. The employers would have to pay the full daily wage to these young workers.

These provisions would go some way towards meeting the International Labour Organisation's mitigation clause on child labour, which states that in an economy which is underdeveloped, and where the provision of education is poor, children may be allowed to do light work. But a definition of what constitutes 'light work' needs to be agreed by all parties involved in the issue of child labour in Bangladesh. There will then need to be rigorous monitoring by factory inspectors and trade unions in the industry.

Protecting young workers

For many years an organisation called Saptagram has recognised that children could be both protected and earn a wage in a factory. Although it works in the districts of Faridpur and Jessore and has a rural base it also operates a silk factory which has offered employment to child workers, especially young girls.

Saptagram tries to help children who are particularly vulnerable, from very poor homes and families where the father was absent. Many such girls were attracting the attention of older men looking for young brides. Under Saptagram's care, they were employed on light tasks like spinning the silk thread, and went to school for part of each day. The girls were able to take a wage home to their mothers, who were then less tempted to 'sell off' their daughters in marriage.

The example of Saptagram and the arguments of NGOs like GSS illustrate the complexities of attempting to address the child labour issue within a Western framework. It is inappropriate to apply Western definitions and principles in a country like Bangladesh. For many poor families, the contribution of children's labour is vital. The tiny amount earned by a child working in a textile factory can make the difference between family survival and disintegration. One such child-worker said bitterly 'if the government does not let me work, let them get my food!' Young girls certainly need the protection of enforceable Factory Acts but they also need money and the degree of freedom it gives them, in a culture which still regards them as second-class citizens.

Ironically, some of the under-age garment workers who are laid off to comply with enforcement of child labour laws will join the hidden production lines of the informal sector. Here, in unregistered back-street workshops, they will receive even lower wages, and have to work in dangerous and unhealthy conditions. Many of these concerns work as sub-contractors to the registered factories. But not all children will find work, and as unemployment increases, wages in the industry are becoming lower.

International markets and governments need to understand the economic situation of child factory workers. Their rights to education and health care need to be recognised, but so does their need for an income.

Looking after the silkworms at Saptagram's silk factory.

Conclusion

The story of Bangladesh is one of endurance and courage. The long colonial history of exploitation and oppression culminated in the devastating War of Liberation in which around two million died. But the war for liberation from poverty and oppression is still continuing.

Bangladesh politics since Independence have been violent and unstable, and a constant struggle has been waged against corruption and dictatorship. The war against oppression is also being fought out in countless small villages, by people who have very few resources except their united determination, against the tyrannical power of landowners, officials, and police. There is also the hidden struggle of women oppressed by patriarchal social structures which deny them power over their own lives. Another fight is taking place in the world arena for fairer terms of trade for emerging industries. Bangladeshis also have to fight repeatedly against their ancient enemies of floods, cyclones, and droughts. They have learned to survive in situations that would totally defeat a less resourceful people.

Independent NGOs, both national and international, work closely with the people and their own grassroots organisations, helping the voiceless to find their voice, and supporting those working for their own empowerment.

These are long-drawn out wars being fought by peaceful means for liberation from oppression, for freedom from poverty, and for social justice and human rights. Despite the internal and external forces ranged against them, the people of Bangladesh still continue to fight for real liberation with an enduring courage.

Oxfam in Bangladesh

Oxfam has worked in Bangladesh since 1971, responding with emergency assistance at times of crisis, and funding local organisations that are seeking long-term solutions to povery and powerlessness. Working through individuals and groups, often in remote areas, Oxfam supports people in their struggle to become self-reliant and to overcome some of the obstacles that keep them in poverty. Most of the people and projects featured in this book have benefited from Oxfam support, and their stories illustrate the fact that a small investment of funds in the right place at the right time can have a profound effect on people's lives.

The main areas of development which Oxfam has funded in Bangladesh are reducing vulnerability to disasters, making the best use of land, education, health care, legal rights, and strengthening community organisations. An important focus of Oxfam's work has been supporting groups of landless people, especially women. Functional education and information on land rights can enable people to take effective action. This work is supported by advocacy on land reform.

As the capacity of the major national NGOs in Bangladesh has grown, Oxfam has focused its support on small and emerging organisations, which often work on a very localised scale. Many of the large, established NGOs started originally with support from Oxfam.

Because of Bangladesh's vulnerability to natural disasters, helping people to prepare against cyclones and floods is an element of all development projects supported by Oxfam, as is the emphasis on building recovery capacity through development.

SHAFIQUL ALAM

Jahanara Khatoon bought this cow with a loan from the women's group in her village. The group has received support and advice from the Community Development Association (CDA), an NGO funded by Oxfam. Besides helping the women to set up a rotating loan scheme, CDA encouraged them to grow vegetables, and provided literacy training and health education. Jahanara has gained in confidence since learning to read, and takes more of a share in decisions within the family now that she is able to make a financial contribution by selling milk from her cow.

Area:	**144,000 square km**
Population:	**120 million**
Population growth rate:	**1.95% per annum**
Population density:	**780 per square km**
Life expectancy:	**55 years**
Male/female ratio:	**106:100**
Average female age at first marriage:	**1974: 15.9 years** **1984: 17.8 years** **1991: 18.2 years**
Infant mortality:	**115 per 1,000 live births (0 - 5 years)**
1 doctor for every:	**5,200 people (UK 1 - 650)**
1 hospital bed for every:	**3,200 people**
Literacy:	**32% of adults (43% of men, 22% of women)**
Religious affiliation:	**87% Muslim, 11% Hindu, 1% Buddhist, 1% Christians and animists**
Principal exports:	**garments, jute and its products, shellfish, tea, and leather.**
Main trading partners:	**US, EU and Japan**
Main aid donors:	**US, UK, Canada, and Japan**
Gross Domestic Product:	**1991 US$23,394m** **1992 US$23,783m** **1993 US$24,050m**
Average annual income:	**US$220 per capita**
Rice production:	**1991 17.8m tonnes** **1992 18.27m tonnes** **1993 18.6m tonnes**

Sources: UNICEF, DTI, Economist Intelligence Unit, World Bank

Sources and further reading

Hartmann B and Boyce J, A *Quiet Violence: View from a Bangladesh Village,*
Zed Press, 1983.

Hartmann B and Standing H, *Food, Saris and Sterilization,*
Bangladesh International Action Group, 1985.

Phelan B *Made in Bangladesh: Women, Garments and the Multi-fibre Arrangement,*
Bangladesh International Action Group, 1986.

Huq S and Rahman A, *Environmental Profile of Bangladesh,*
Bangladesh Centre for Environmental Studies, 1987.

BMSP, *State of Human Rights in Bangladesh 1993,*
Coordinating Council for Human Rights in Bangladesh, Dhaka, 1993.

Hughes H, Adnan S & Dalal-Clayton B, *Floodplains or Flood Plans,*
International Institute for Environment and Development, London and Research and
Advisory Services, Dhaka, 1994.

Quddus M, *Entrepreneurship in Apparel Export Industry of Bangladesh,*
Unpublished Research Paper, University of Southern Indiana, Evansville In, 1993.

White S, *Arguing with the Crocodile,*
ZED Books Ltd, London and University Press, Dhaka, 1992.

UNDP, *Empowerment of Women,*
United Nations Development Programme, Dhaka, 1994.

UNICEF, *The Fork in the Path,*
UNICEF, Foundation, Dhaka, 1994.

Wood G D, *Bangladesh: Whose Ideas, Whose Interests?*
Intermediate Technology Publications, 1994.

IMAGES OF WA

THE WAFFEN-SS ARDENNES OFFENSIVE

RARE PHOTOGRAPHS FROM WARTIME ARCHIVES

Ian Baxter

Pen & Sword
MILITARY

First published in Great Britain in 2022 by
PEN & SWORD MILITARY
an imprint of Pen & Sword Books Ltd
Yorkshire – Philadelphia

ISBN 978-1-39901-289-8

Typeset by Concept, Huddersfield, West Yorkshire, HD4 5JL.
Printed and bound in England by CPI Group (UK) Ltd, Croydon CR0 4YY.

Pen & Sword Books Limited incorporates the imprints of Atlas, Archaeology, Aviation, Discovery, Family History, Fiction, History, Maritime, Military, Military Classics, Politics, Select, Transport, True Crime, Air World, Frontline Publishing, Leo Cooper, Remember When, Seaforth Publishing, The Praetorian Press, Wharncliffe Local History, Wharncliffe Transport, Wharncliffe True Crime and White Owl.

For a complete list of Pen & Sword titles please contact
PEN & SWORD BOOKS LTD
47 Church Street, Barnsley, South Yorkshire, S70 2AS, England
E-mail: enquiries@pen-and-sword.co.uk
Website: www.pen-and-sword.co.uk
or
PEN & SWORD BOOKS
1950 Lawrence Rd, Havertown, PA 19083, USA
E-mail: uspen-and-sword@casematepublishers.com
Website: www.penandswordbooks.com

Introduction

Thrown back by massive Soviet assaults, Hitler's only way to escape annihilation was to win a quick peace with the Allies in the West by launching a devastating surprise attack through the Ardennes. Utilizing his premier Waffen-SS divisions as the backbone for this attack, he hoped that these elite formations would smash the enemy front lines through the densely-forested regions of eastern Belgium, France and Luxembourg and stop the Allied use of the Belgian port of Antwerp, splitting the Allied lines, and allowing its units to encircle and destroy four Allied armies.

This book, with its extensive text and rare and unpublished photographs with detailed captions, tells the story of the Waffen-SS offensive, known as *Wacht am Rhein* (Watch on the Rhine). It describes how these formidable SS units with their supporting Wehrmacht divisions drove back their enemy, sending their powerful armour along the twisting narrow roads and mountainous terrain, capturing villages and towns as they advanced. However, their forces were steadily ground down by mounting losses and lack of supplies and fuel. Hindered by terrible winter weather together with the unyielding resistance of their enemy, it culminated in the loss of the Battle of Bastogne. As a result, the Waffen-SS were reluctantly withdrawn and the remnants of this foremost fighting machine transferred back to the Eastern Front to deal with another growing threat.

The Führer's Plan

In September 1944, as Adolf Hitler lay in his sick bed at his East Prussian head-quarters, *Wolfsschanze* ('The Wolf's Lair'), his depression lifted as he envisaged not another defensive line but a far bolder campaign: a great offensive in the West. Excitedly, he called for his chief of Wehrmacht operations, General Alfred Jodl, who came to Hitler's bunker bedroom with a map which they then spread out on the bed. In a voice familiar from what he considered to be his old days of triumph, Hitler told Jodl that he had decided to launch a great winter counterattack in the West through the Ardennes, the scene of his 1940 victory, and capture the town of Antwerp. 'Fog, night and snow' would be on his side. With Antwerp in German hands, he predicted that both the British and American forces would have no port from which to escape and subsequently a new Dunkirk would emerge, but this time the enemy would not be allowed to escape. Although the proposal at first seemed too adventurous to his war staff, he was once more exhibiting an energy and enthusiasm that he had not shown for some time. Despite the fact that almost a million German soldiers had been lost since the Allied invasion of France, many generals would never have conceived that a nation so close to decimation could perform or even consider such a plan, which Hitler hoped would stop the Western Allies and allow him to switch his strength to the East and so save Germany from complete devastation.

To ensure absolute secrecy about the forthcoming offensive, only a handful of those who were directly involved were told of the daring plan. Not even the generals commanding the army groups on either side of the Ardennes sector were to know about the coming attacks. Nothing connected to the offensive was to be transmitted by teletype or telephone. Officers, sworn to silence, would be used as couriers. At all costs Allied intelligence was also not allowed to have the slightest suspicion that the new forces the Germans were raising were going to attack the Ardennes. Hitler was determined to achieve complete surprise. Within three months of drafting the first plans for the Ardennes offensive, Hitler had moved to a new headquarters in Germany, nicknamed *Adlerhorst* ('Eagle's Nest'), so that he could be nearer to the Western Front.

General Wilhelm Keitel, with the aid of a map, outlines plans to Hitler during a military situation conference. General Alfred Jodl can also be seen in attendance at the meeting. Hitler's plan for launching a devastating surprise attack through the Ardennes also surprised his war staff. Utilizing his premier Waffen-SS divisions as the backbone for the attack, he hoped that these elite formations would smash the enemy front lines through the densely-forested regions of eastern Belgium, France and Luxembourg and stop Allied use of the Belgian port of Antwerp, splitting the Allied lines, and allow his units to encircle and destroy four Allied armies.

On 11 and 12 December, just days before the attack, he summoned his Western Front commanders to confer in a secret meeting. Because Hitler was so obsessed with security leaks, every man at war conferences was asked to sign a document swearing him to utter secrecy. In a two-hour lecture to the sixty or so assembled commanders, Hitler revealed the political and military motives for deciding upon the offensive. Although they were astounded, they all listened, some impressed not only by the grandiosity of the plan but by his vigour and determination.

The Main Commanders

General Field Marshal Walther Model. Model was known as the 'Führer's troubleshooter'. As a result of his energy and brilliance on the battlefield he saw much success on the Eastern Front in 1944. It was here during bitter battles against strong Russian attacks that Model first introduced the 'Shield and Sword' policy, which stated that retreats were intolerable unless they paved the way for a counterstroke later. Out on the battlefield he not only continued to be energetic, courageous and innovative but was friendly and popular with his enlisted men. He brought the same energy and enthusiasm when he became commander of Army Group B in Normandy and then in Holland during the Battle of Arnhem. However, for the planned Ardennes offensive where Model resumed command of Army Group B, he believed, along with all the other commanders, that the operation was unachievable given the resources available to the Wehrmacht and Waffen-SS on the Western Front at such a late point in the war. He did think at the same time that the offensive would delay Germany's defeat but not prevent it.

Field Marshal Model can be seen conversing with frontline commanders with the aid of a map. In spite of being a brilliant commander who was respected by both the Wehrmacht and Waffen-SS, he believed the offensive was unachievable given the fact that it was so late in the war.

General Hasso Eccard von Manteuffel. Manteuffel was a panzer expert and saw much success on the Eastern Front. In 1944 he was appointed commander of the *Grossdeutschland* Division where he directed operations across the Ukraine and then saw action in Army Group North. On 1 September 1944 he was promoted to general of panzer troops and given command of the 5th Panzer Army on the Western Front. It was here along the German border that the army saw heavy combat against Allied forces, with his armour suffering heavily from both Allied air and ground attack. In November Manteuffel was instructed to prepare his 5th Panzer Army and move into Belgium to form up in the Ardennes alongside the newly-formed 6th SS Panzer Army.

SS-Oberstgruppenführer Josef 'Sepp' Dietrich. Dietrich had been a successful commander since 1939 when he commanded the *SS-Leibstandarte* during the German advance into Poland and later the Netherlands, Greece and Yugoslavia. As a dedicated and enthusiastic commander, his successes in the field saw him later given command of the 1st SS Panzer Corps in 1943 on the Eastern Front. He then took his panzer corps to Normandy where it oversaw operations; then he was further promoted and given command of the 5th Panzer Army and then the 6th Panzer Army. Following the armies' withdrawal across France, Dietrich was then ordered in November 1944 to prepare his army and move it to the Ardennes.

(**Above, left**) *SS-Gruppenführer* Hermann Priess. A ruthless and brutal commander, Priess was given command of the SS *Totenkopf* Division following death of Theodor Eicke in February 1943. Following considerable success and his tactics with his armoured units, in October 1944 Priess succeeded George Keppler as commander of I SS Panzer Corps. A few weeks later he was ordered to assemble his panzer corps and move it to the Ardennes where he led this formation as part of the 6th Panzer Army.

(**Above, right**) *SS-Obergruppenführer* Wilhelm Bittrich. Bittrich's skill and obstinacy as an SS military tactician distinguished him as a commander in the field and earned him temporary command of the 2nd SS Panzer Division *Das Reich* in late 1941 after the division's commander Paul Hausser had been wounded. He then was given command over the 9th SS Panzer Division *Hohenstaufen* in 1943 for a year. On 1 July 1944, he was appointed commander of II SS Panzer Corps which fought in Normandy and then later in September at Arnhem. As soon as the battle had ended *Hohenstaufen*, which had suffered heavy losses, was immediately removed and departed from the area for its long-awaited rest and refit in Paderborn. Weeks later Bittrich was given the order to move his corps to prepare for the Ardennes offensive.

(**Right**) General Erich Brandenberger. He commanded the 8th Panzer Division February 1941 to January 1943. He then went on to assume command of LIX Army Corps and then XXIX Army Corps on the Eastern Front. As a dedicated and enthusiastic commander, his successes in the field saw him given command in late 1944 of the 7th Army on the Western Front, where he would direct his new force through the Ardennes.

General Gustav-Adolf von Zangen. Von Zangen quickly went through the ranks as a dedicated, loyal and determined officer. He commanded the 17th Infantry Division, took part in operations on the Eastern Front and soon earned men's respect. He then commanded an army detachment in Italy in 1943 and was later appointed commander of the 15th Army on the Western Front. Following an evacuation of France in the summer of 1944, his army withdrew across the Scheldt to the Island of Walcheren and South Beveland. It was here between October and November that his divisions were attacked and bombed by the Allies. In November he was instructed to prepare his divisions for operations in the Ardennes and move out all units that were resting in Holland.

Main Waffen-SS Units used for the Ardennes Offensive

1st SS Panzer Division
Leibstandarte

2nd SS Panzer Division
Das Reich

9th SS Panzer Division
Hohenstaufen

12th SS Panzer Division
Hitlerjugend

1st SS Panzer Division Leibstandarte

Commander: *SS-Brigadeführer* Wilhelm Mohnke.

Following action in Normandy, in December 1944 the LSSAH found itself being employed for action in the Ardennes. Along with a number of re-formed Waffen-SS formations, units of the *Leibstandarte* were converted into smaller, fast-moving *Kampfgruppen* (battle groups). The LSSAH was attached to the I SS Panzer Corps and was to spearhead the operation.

Kampfgruppe Peiper
(part of the 1st SS Panzer Division)

Commander: *SS-Obersturmführer* Joachim Peiper.

For the Ardennes offensive within the 6th Panzer Army, a new mobile strike role was assigned to the *SS-Leibstandarte*. The division was split into four combined-arms battle groups with one most famously known as *Kampfgruppe Peiper*, which commanded the most substantial group, which included all armoured sections of the division. *Peiper* also received the 501st Heavy Panzer Battalion with the new 70-ton King Tiger tanks. Main armoured vehicles used in the *Kampfgruppe* consisted of Pz.Kpfw.IV Ausf.H, Pz.Kpfw.V Ausf.G Panthers, Pz.Kpfw.VI Tigers, Pz.Kpfw.VI Ausf.B King Tigers, Bison Ausf.M Sd.Kfz.138/1 150mm sIG 33/2 howitzer carriers (rear-mounted) and *Wirbelwinds*.

(**Above, left**) *SS-Brigadeführer* Wilhelm Mohnke commanded the SS Division *Leibstandarte* and participated in the fighting in France, Poland and the Balkans. In 1943 he was appointed to command a regiment in the SS Division *Hitlerjugend* where he led his unit in the defence of Caen in Normandy, where he received a Knight's Cross of the Iron Cross. Within months Mohnke was given command again of his original division, the *Leibstandarte*, for a new offensive on the Western Front in the Ardennes.

(**Above, right**) *SS-Obersturmführer* Joachim Peiper was initially Heinrich Himmler's adjutant. However, during the campaign against France in 1940, he obtained permission to join a combat unit and became a platoon leader within the *Leibstandarte*, in which role he excelled. It was not until later in the war that Peiper joined the *Leibstandarte* on the Eastern Front. During the Battle of Kharkov in March 1943, Peiper showed his skill and tenacity on the battlefield as a commander, but also earned a reputation of being merciless, both to the enemy and to innocent civilians. Also his command style was aggressive and without regard for casualties of his own men. Yet Hitler regarded Peiper as the type of commander that would yield success in the Ardennes and in November 1944, after convalescing in a Bavarian hospital following a nervous breakdown, he was given command of a *Kampfgruppe*, the most powerful mobile strike force within the SS *Leibstandarte*. It was named *Kampfgruppe Peiper*.

(**Opposite, above**) Soldiers of the *Leibstandarte* in action on the Eastern Front, probably in 1943. Note the divisional symbol painted on the rear of the ammunition trailer for the *FlaK* gun mounted on the half-track.

(**Opposite, below**) Troops and armour of *Kampfgruppe Peiper* moving forward towards their assembly area along a muddy road. Though it is often not documented, mud was a constant hindrance to armour and soldiers in the Ardennes. As in Russia, rain and thawing snow often turned tracks and roads into a quagmire, slowing down columns.

2nd SS Panzer Division Das Reich

Commander: *SS-Gruppenführer* Heinz Lammerding.

The division had been recuperating and refitting in Sauerland following its high losses in the Normandy campaign. It was ordered westward, where it was to take part in the Ardennes offensive. Although the movement order of the division to cross the Rhine was issued on 11 November, it was not until the 24th that the last contingents of the divisional units reached the western bank. Once it arrived in Belgium, parts of the division were broken into *Kampfgruppen* in order to defend corps flanks against possible attack.

(**Below, left**) *SS-Gruppenführer* Heinz Lammerding became commander of the SS *Das Reich* Division in January 1944. He was a staunch Nazi, but was not considered by many officers under his command to be a military strategist. In fact, his chief of staff and regimental commanders were required to come up with battle plans and it was Lammerding who took credit for their success. However, his political views and his ruthless and callous nature gave him the opportunity to lead a premier SS division in Normandy and then the Ardennes.

(**Below, centre**) *SS-Brigadeführer* Sylvester Stadler during a command on the Eastern Front. In 1944 Stadler was panzergrenadier regiment commander of *Der Führer* of the *Das Reich* Division. He was then given command of the 9th SS *Hohenstaufen* Division from 10 July until he was relieved of his command on 31 July 1944, only having the position for three weeks. Ironically, he was then again given the command of the division in October of that year and was tasked with commanding his division through the Ardennes.

(**Below, right**) *SS-Obersturmbannführer* Hugo Kraas saw action in the SS *Leibstandarte* in Poland, Holland, the Balkans and on the Eastern Front. His cold-blooded nature and merciless approach to his men in the face of adversity saw him receive the German Cross in Gold for distinction on the battlefield. In November 1944 he was given command of what was known in Normandy as the *Baby Division*, the 12th SS Panzer Division *Hitlerjugend*. In late November the division was sent to the Ardennes.

Soldiers of the *Das Reich* Division utilizing a bombed-out crater, probably during operations in Normandy in the summer of 1944.

9th SS Panzer Division

Commander: *SS-Brigadeführer* Sylvester Stadler.

The 9th SS saw extensive action in the Arnhem area in Holland in September 1944. As soon as the battle had ended *Hohenstaufen*, which had suffered since fighting in Holland started, was no longer capable of offensive action. For this reason it was immediately removed and departed from the area in order for its long-awaited rest and refit in the Reich at Paderborn. Only a few weeks later the division was ordered to the west again, this time to the Ardennes where on 12 December 1944 they moved south to Münstereifel. It was to act as a reserve for Sepp Dietrich's 6th SS Panzer Army.

12th SS Panzer Division Hitlerjugend

Commander: *SS-Standartenführer* Hugo Kraas.

Following heavy fighting in Normandy in November 1944, the division was sent to Nienburg in Germany to recuperate, refit and be re-formed. The majority of reinforcements were transferred from Luftwaffe and Kriegsmarine personnel. Its commander Hubert Meyer was replaced by *SS-Obersturmbannführer* Hugo Kraas, and the division was attached to the 6th SS Panzer Army of *SS-Oberstgruppenführer* Sepp Dietrich, which was forming up for operations in the Ardennes.

Soldiers of the 9th SS *Hohenstaufen* during operations in the relief of German forces trapped in the Kamenets-Podolsky Pocket on the Eastern Front. The division went on to fight in Normandy and Arnhem, and was then sent to the Ardennes in early December 1944.

In Normandy, a young *Hitlerjugend* soldier clad in his summer SS camouflage smock and armed with an MG42. By early December the division began moving into its assembly area in the Ardennes.

Chapter One

Preparation and Assembly

On 10 November 1944, Hitler issued the 'Order' for assembly and preparation for attack. The following day Supreme Command West issued the order for the offensive to Army Group B. For preparations, all available resources and even divisions initially destined for the Eastern Front were pulled back and diverted to the Ardennes area for further orders.

For the attack in the Ardennes, Field Marshal Walther Model's Army Group B, which contained four armies, was the force chosen to play the major role. The 15th Army, however, was not to take part in the operations but the three other armies in Model's army group were prepared for action. This included the 6th Panzer Army, *General der Panzertruppen* Hasso von Manteuffel's 5th Panzer Army and *General der Panzertruppen* Erich Brandenberger's 7th Army. All three armies were to attack the American positions between Monschau in the north and Echternach in the south. The force was to drive through the American VIII Corps and advance at full speed for the River Meuse to the rear of that corps. Once this mighty army had crossed the river, they would then head for the capital, Brussels, and the massive supply base at Antwerp.

For operations in the Ardennes a substantial number of Waffen-SS divisions were assigned to the area, including four crack divisions. These premier Waffen-SS units were paramount to the success of the offensive and regarded as the backbone of the attack. These SS divisions were larger than the regular Wehrmacht Panzer divisions and totalled a ground strength of between 16,000 and 20,000 soldiers, with three-battalion Panzergrenadier regiments, a slightly larger artillery regiment that included a battalion of *Nebelwerfers* and a *Sturmgeschütz Abteilung* with twenty or thirty assault guns. The SS also had a higher allotment of motor vehicles. However, they were still below their assigned strength of officers and non-commissioned officers, mostly because of the terrible losses sustained in Normandy.

The equipment that was assigned to the SS armoured formations for the offensive was generally excellent, although by this late period of the war it was still in short supply. The forces committed to the battle zone contained a number of independent self-propelled anti-tank and heavy tank battalions and several assault gun brigades, which were battalion-size formations. There were four *Schwere Panzerjäger* battalions, nominally equipped with a mix of *Jagdpanthers*, *Panzerjäger* IVs and *Sturmgeschütz* IIIs. The *Schwere* Panzer battalions contained the famous Tiger heavy tanks. Three of these units were committed in the Ardennes and the powerful 501st SS *Schwere Panzer Abteilung* was hastily dispatched to the area.

As the final plans were put into motion, the SS units marched into their assembly areas along with their Wehrmacht counterparts. All movement was undertaken at night without using any vehicle lights. Even brake lights were covered. The march for the troops was made more difficult by the roads, which were narrow and icy. Due to congestion of the small winding roads, commanders marched the SS in blocks to reduce the traffic situation and lessen the possibility of the enemy detecting movement.

During the nights of 13/14 and 15 December the bulk of these units were moved to their assembly points. This included the main element of the SS comprising *SS-Oberstgruppenführer* Josef 'Sepp' Dietrich's panzers which consisted of I SS Panzer Corps, whose principal components were the 1st SS Panzer Division LSAH and the 12th SS Panzer Division *Hitlerjugend*. The 12th SS had been refitting in the region of Cologne in November and had been ordered to move to Belgium where it was deployed along the front in the Hollerath sector along with the 1st SS Panzer Division. In reserve supporting the I SS was the II SS Panzer Corps, comprising the 2nd SS Panzer Division *Das Reich* and the 9th SS Panzer Division *Hohenstaufen*.

The most powerful SS formation that was to spearhead the attack through the Ardennes was to be formed by I SS Panzer Corps. It was tasked with punching a massive hole in the American lines between Hollerath and Krewinkel and drive through to the Liege-Huy area with the *Hitlerjugend* supporting its right flank and the LSAH on the left.

The drive through these twisting narrow roads was not going to be easy, but the task of leading the attack of the powerful I SS Panzer Corps was given to the commander of the 6th SS Panzer Army, *SS-Obersturmführer* Joachim Peiper. The divisions in this army were to be split into four combined-arms battle groups or *Kampfgruppen*, with Peiper commanding the most substantial. The *Kampfgruppen* included all armoured sections of the division. Peiper also received the 501st SS *Schwere Panzer Abteilung* with the new 70-ton Tiger II or King Tiger tanks, as they were referred to.

To the south of the 6th Panzer Army's sector lay *General der Panzertruppen* von Manteuffel's 5th Panzer Army and General Erich Brandenberger's 7th Army, which was the southernmost of the three armies committed to the offensive. Altogether the five Panzer and Panzergrenadier divisions and thirteen infantry-type divisions consisting of *Fallschirmjäger* and *Volksgrenadier* troops were to be unleashed through the Belgian and Luxembourg countryside.

With all these divisions prepared to do battle, there was still great concern that the assembly areas of such a large number of troops might not go unnoticed by the enemy. Although the Americans did detect increased traffic activity and refugees reporting a huge equipment build-up in the surrounding woods and forests, there was not enough time to make further reconnaissance. In fact, the Germans had purposely moved many of their units to the assembly areas just before the offensive was to be unleashed.

Within twenty-four hours of the attack, large numbers of trains with their special flat beds loaded with Tiger tanks and other armour were rushed to the assembly areas. These included searchlights and masses of other matériel required for the divisions. In fact, some of the units arrived in their allocated area a couple of hours before H-hour in order to attain absolute secrecy.

The new Tiger II or King Tiger tanks can be seen here on board special flatbed rail cars destined for the front. These King Tigers were issued to heavy tank battalions or *Schwere Panzer Abteilung* on the basis of forty-five of them being employed in each battalion. They were divided into three companies of fourteen Tiger IIs each (a total of forty-two), with the remaining three allocated to battalion headquarters. Each platoon of tanks was supposed to consist of three to four tanks.

(**Above**) A late-variant Pz.Kpfw.IV still retaining its Eastern Front whitewash camouflage paint can be seen here negotiating its way over a pontoon bridge. During the winter of 1944–45, the Panzer IV was one of the most numerous tanks in the Ardennes offensive.

(**Opposite, above**) A column of Panther tanks still retaining their summer camouflage scheme from France. A status report on 15 December 1944, a day before the attack in the Ardennes, listed that some 471 Panthers had been assigned to the Western Front, with 336 operational. Some 400 Panthers in the report stated that these were employed on the Western Front and were assigned in units sent to the Ardennes.

(**Opposite, below**) A column of Tiger IIs advancing to their assembly area. Between the end of September and late November 1944, *Schwere Panzer Abteilung* 501 received these Tigers. The first ten Tiger IIs arrived in October, with another twenty-four arriving in November. Eleven more Tiger IIs were issued, handed over by *Schwere Panzer Abteilung* 509 at the beginning of December as the unit prepared to take part in the Ardennes offensive.

Two grenadiers resting. The soldier on the right is armed with the MP 40 machine gun. Both men are wearing the standard infantryman's greatcoat.

An MG42 winter-clad gun crew during a pause in the fighting share a cigarette. (NARA)

A typical German dugout along the front. Although unable to sustain heavy systematic bombardments from the enemy, these positions offered the men some degree of shelter from the rain and cold weather. Many hundreds of these dugouts were built along the front as the troops assembled and were commonly known by the Germans as 'small houses'.

Soldiers in their assembly areas preparing their positions in readiness for the attack. It was not until mid to late November 1944 that troops began slowly assembling in their allocated areas, hidden in the forests and densely-wooded terrain of the Ardennes.

Two grenadiers are seen preparing a shelter using pine logs from the surrounding forest. (NARA)

A commanding officer holding the rank of *SS-Obersturmführer* can be seen conferring with his men on a muddy road. A column of support vehicles carrying supplies to the front has halted. Note the soldier on the far left of the photograph. He is a military policeman or *Feldgendarmerie*. He wears the standard German greatcoat with the dull aluminium gorget plate suspended around his neck by a chain. He has more than likely been tasked to direct the traffic to its assembly areas.

(**Opposite, above**) Infantry dismount from a truck in a muddy field and will move off to their allocated area. Once in their assembly zone, they will be briefed and given strict orders to remain vigilant and quiet until further instructions are received.

(**Opposite, below**) Troops preparing their positions in a wooded area. They all wear their reversible winter parka grey-side-out.

(**Above**) In a wooded area a machine-gunner clad in a greatcoat can be seen here armed with an MG 42 slung over his shoulder for ease of carriage.

(**Above**) An Sd.Kfz.10 mounting a *FlaK* gun on a road destined for the front. A special platform with fold-down side and rear panels can be seen here. This platform was specifically designed for the *FlaK* mount and allowed the crew to operate the gun.

(**Opposite**) A stationary Sd.Kfz.251 half-track with some of the crew members conversing. A washing line has been erected between two trees and the crew's underwear can be seen hung across the line to dry. Note the M35 steel helmets attached to the vehicle's side armour in order to give it better armoured protection. The Sd.Kfz.251 was used extensively during the latter half of the war to transport panzergrenadiers to the forward edge of the battlefield. Despite being in the main lightly armoured, they could maintain a relatively modest speed, manoeuvre across country and keep up with the fast-moving spearheads.

(**Below**) A 15cm gun crew can be seen posing for the camera in front of their well-camouflaged gun. The barrel is elevated and prepared for a fire mission. Preparatory bombardment against American lines was key to the successful advance of the SS through the Ardennes.

In the Ardennes in early December 1944 showing commanding officers inside a Volkswagen Type 166 *Schwimm-wagen*, which literally means floating/swimming car. This amphibious four-wheel-drive off-roader was used extensively by both the Wehrmacht and Waffen-SS on the Western Front. The Type 166 was the most numerous mass-produced amphibious car in history.

A smiling grenadier wearing his reversible parka grey-side-out. *(NARA)*

(**Above**) An Sd.Kfz.250 can be seen in a field as panzergrenadiers pass on their way to the battlefront. The soldiers are wearing various combinations of the Wehrmacht reversible two-piece winter suit.

(**Right**) A grenadier drinks from his canteen prior to going into action.

(**Opposite, above**) A *Sturmgeschütz* III stationary on a road. For the Ardennes, anti-tank battalions were modified, making them more or less motorized and comprising an anti-tank company equipped with *Jagdpanzer* IVs, Hetzers or *StuGs* and supported by a motorized anti-tank company of PaK and FlaK guns.

(**Opposite, below**) These grenadiers appear to have requisitioned a building on a farmstead and are pictured having emerged from it. Outside is a parked Sd.Kfz.251 half-track. A typical panzergrenadier division had at least one battalion of infantry that were transported to the forward edge of the battlefield by Sd.Kfz.251 half-tracks and various armoured support provided by its own StuG battalion. A typical panzergrenadier division normally comprised an HQ company, a motorized engineer battalion and two panzergrenadier regiments.

Chapter Two

Attack (Watch on the Rhine)

The code-name for the Ardennes offensive was *Wacht am Rhein* (Watch on the Rhine), and it was planned to begin in the early morning of 16 December 1944. On the eve of the offensive, Hitler held a final conference and received reports confirming a forecast of several days of bad weather, which would ground enemy aircraft. That evening he dined with his secretaries, and as he retired to bed at five in the morning, a few hundred miles away to the north-west thousands of troops attacked simultaneously along a weak 85-mile sector of the 450 miles of the British-American front. Hitler's last gamble in the west had begun.

All along the German front, from Monschau in the north to Echternach on the Luxembourg border, the cold dawn of 16 December was broken by the shouts of German gunnery officers giving the orders for their men to begin a massive artillery barrage. Across the rolling hills, dense pine forests, deeply cut ravines and narrow roads the Ardennes erupted in a wall of flame and smoke. Some 2,000 light, medium and heavy guns, howitzers and *Nebelwerfers* poured fire and destruction onto enemy positions. Shell after shell thundered into American strongpoints. Some American soldiers, fearing complete annihilation, scrambled from their sleeping bags and threw themselves into shelters and foxholes.

In the north the 6th Panzer Army inflicted the heaviest barrage of fire. At least 657 guns and howitzers and 340 *Nebelwerfers* were directed on American positions between Höfen and the Losheim Gap. For almost an hour without interruption, shells screamed over the heads of the waiting German infantry. Abruptly the bombardment ended, leaving a stunned silence for a few moments. Then beneath the pines and camouflage netting, thousands of German soldiers began their attack.

SS-Oberstgruppenführer Stadtinger, who commanded the artillery of the 6th SS Panzer Army, described his firepower:

> Besides the divisional artillery of both Corps, we had one battalion of three batteries, each with nine guns ranging from 150mm to 210mm. In Army artillery we had two nine-barrelled mortar [*Nebelwerfer*] brigades plus three brigades of heavy artillery, 200mm, 240mm and 350mm. We also had two or three *Volks-artillerie* Corps of six battalions each.

Almost all over the front, except from one part of Manteuffel's sector, shell after shell thundered into American strongpoints.

At first, Allied commanders were unable to discover the full extent of the attack because German guns had succeeded, within a few minutes, in severing telephone communications between all the American commands. One American journalist wrote that 'With the exception of Pearl Harbor, never had American troops been thrown into greater confusion by an attack as that mounted in December 1944.' In the north, the 6th SS Panzer Army, commanded by Sepp Dietrich, inflicted the heaviest barrage of fire. All along the front SS artillery, tanks and Panzergrenadiers fired on command posts and road crossings and blasted their way through villages and along narrow twisting roads.

Supporting these powerful Waffen-SS units were *Volksgrenadiers*, many going into battle for the first time. Prior to battle, a number of them had openly expressed that they were excited at the thought of fighting an offensive that their Führer had said would drive the invaders from their homeland and win the greatest victory since Dunkirk. Advancing across fields, along roads and hills, the *Volksgrenadiers* advanced in close formation with tanks from the crack SS Panzer divisions, which were blasting their way through enemy lines. The 277th *Volksgrenadier* Division attacked well with units of the 12th *SS-Hitlerjugend* on the right and the *SS-Leibstandarte* on the left. The main spearhead in the region towards Losheimergraben was undertaken by the *SS-Leibstandarte*. Although the 277th *Volksgrenadier* Division successfully fought its way through American lines, by the afternoon of the offensive it made no headway and had to rely on the SS to pull it through.

Along other parts of the front from the 6th SS Panzer Army in the north to General Brandenberger's 7th Army in the south, the attack was showing signs of considerable success, with lines being burst open and enemy units either being surrounded or driven from their burning positions. In order to further confuse the enemy, *SS-Obersturmbannführer* Otto Skorzeny's *SS-Jagdkommmando* (Hunting Commando) of the 150th Panzer Brigade was sent out primarily as saboteurs. This special unit, which was Hitler's idea, comprised some 2,000 English-speaking German Commandos who were well-trained saboteurs dressed in American uniforms and using captured American jeeps. They were pushed far ahead of the main German advance, cutting telephone communications, turning and whitewashing signposts, setting up minefield indicators and creating as much confusion behind enemy lines as possible.

The sudden speed and depth of the German attack through the Ardennes was a brilliant display of all-arms coordination. For the first time in many months, the offensive had given each soldier an aura of invincibility that had not been enjoyed since the early years of the war. As for the American defenders, the troops were quite unprepared for the might of the German 5th and 6th Panzer armies and were simply brushed aside. US troops were totally caught off guard, lulled into a false sense of security by the previous weeks of inactivity along the 'rest' front. They had been told by their commanders that the 'Krauts' were finished and that victory was just around the corner. They might even be home for Christmas. Now they were being attacked and were unable to mount and organize any type of proper cohesive defence. In total confusion, many units retreated to the west. In the Schnee Eifel near St. Vith, the Germans opened heavy concentrated fire on American infantry of the 160th Infantry Division and surrounded them, causing terrible casualties. Further south, five German divisions almost totally destroyed the 28th Division. The 58th and 47th Panzer Corps made strong progress. The 58th Corps crossed the River Ourthe and pushed towards Houffalize to attempt to secure a bridgehead over the Meuse between the Ardennes and Namur. Everywhere it seemed that Panzers were exploiting the difficult terrain. Apart from the old reliable Pz.Kpfw.IV tanks, a number of Panthers were used. The lumbering 70-ton King Tiger tanks and the monster Tiger II Panzers (*Jagdtigers*) were also used, but were so heavy that they were confined to main roads or ground that was frozen solid. It was therefore imperative that all the few good roads had to be seized as quickly as possible, not only for the use of their own armour but to prevent the Americans pouring reinforcements into the area from north to south.

In order to control this network of roads, four communication centres were to be captured and held at all costs: Malmedy, St. Vith, Houffalize and Bastogne. For this huge operation, Hitler's loyal SS Commander Dietrich took and led the most important objectives. To the Americans, it soon became evident that a major offensive was developing, but the elements and the location of the main effort were still far from clear. From their positions around the smaller town of St. Vith, American soldiers watched with fascination as columns of *Volksgrenadiers* and SS soldiers shouted and screamed as they moved forward, attacking. In the distance, panzers were identified supporting the advance. Totally surprised by the advancing German formations, the American soldiers wasted no time and opened up with every available weapon at their disposal. The Germans returned fire using multiple rocket mortars with frightening effect.

A few miles north of St. Vith, in the village of Manderfeld, the American 14th Calvary Group, which guarded the link between the 99th and 106th divisions, was also receiving a hammering from the advancing Germans. Here soldiers were not only dealing with grenadiers of the 18th *Volksgrenadier* Division but also the advance guard of the elite *Kampfgruppe Peiper* of the I SS Panzer Division *Leibstandarte*. Peiper had been a ruthless tanker battalion commander in Russia and allegedly his battalion burned a village to the ground, killing all the inhabitants. The same ruthless streak was also to mark the march of *Kampfgruppe Peiper* across the Ardennes. At his disposal he had about a hundred Pz.Kpfw.IV tanks and Panthers including a battalion of forty-two King Tigers. The 3rd Battalion of the 2nd SS Panzergrenadier Regiment was totally equipped with armoured self-propelled guns, providing Peiper's *Kampfgruppe* with strong infantry support.

In the village and surrounding areas, gunfire, shells from tanks and mortar bombs from the *Volksgrenadiers* and Peiper's men turned Manderfeld into a cauldron of fire and smoke. In the panic and confusion, one American soldier watched a woman scream in agony as both her legs were blown clean off by an explosion: 'We could each see the thigh bone through the bloody gore, her face raked with pain and misery. Besides her lay her three dead children.' Inside Manderfeld, disheartened, frightened American soldiers needed no encouragement to escape the bloodbath. As the sound of German tank tracks approached the village, the Americans quickly took to their heels, clogging the already congested roads. Vehicles that ran out of fuel were simply abandoned. Heavy equipment was dumped by the roadside so that the men could move westward faster, but even here, along the roads between St. Vith and Honsfeld, there was no escape from the slaughter. The town of Honsfeld had been a rest area for the 394th Regiment of the US 99th Infantry Division. Fearing they would be cut off and destroyed by the advancing enemy, many soldiers began fleeing the town. Within hours of the first bombardments, Peiper's Panthers moved into its streets. An American soldier wrote: 'As the Krauts entered the town, we saw paratroopers clinging to the sides of partially camouflaged tanks. Within the crackle of fire these boys jumped off and like wolves attacked anything that moved.' In the confusion that gripped Honsfeld, some Americans fled, others were killed and the rest were left surrounded. It was here that Peiper's men began their trail of massacres by murdering nineteen American soldiers who had capitulated. On that same day, at a crossroads at Baugnez near Malmedy, along the advancing northern wing of Peiper's *Kampfgruppe*, another massacre took place. During a short battle between a number of American armoured vehicles and a column of Peiper's tanks and half-tracks, approximately 125 soldiers of Battery B of the American 285th Field Artillery Observation Battalion were captured and herded into an open field. Hanstholm Siptrott, the commander of Panzer 731, was then ordered to open fire on the prisoners. The wounded that tried to crawl away were shot through the head at point-blank range. At least eighty-six prisoners were killed, but some survived the slaughter by feigning death and later escaped to tell their story.

By this time Peiper had already reported that he was running low on fuel and was compelled to divert his tanks towards Büllingen and capture an American fuel dump there. This consequently allowed his force time to replenish their thirsty Tigers before moving on to capture Schoppen, Ondenval and Thirimont. The *Kampfgruppe* then advanced on Ligneuville, where it met fierce resistance from American troops supported by Sherman tanks. Following its successful capture, Peiper set up a command post in the town while the rest of his *Kampfgruppe* moved on towards Trois-Ponts and Beaumont. At Stavelot the *Kampfgruppe* met strong enemy resistance and were compelled to withdraw for the night and wait for the arrival of Peiper the following morning before resuming the attack. The following day under the command of Peiper the SS once again attacked and captured the bridge at Stavelot intact, and then moved into the town, clearing out all enemy resistance. The *Kampfgruppe* then pressed on towards Trois-Ponts, but was forced to divert its forces because the Americans had succeeded in blowing the bridge over the Amblève river.

By 19 December, Peiper had reached Stoumont, where a vicious two-hour battle raged with Americans trying at all costs to hold the town. When the town could no longer be held the Americans quickly retreated, but Peiper's tanks pursued them for a few miles out of the town before eight of their own tanks were brought to a flaming halt at an American roadblock.

On the morning of 20 December Supreme Command West reported the current situation. It noted that the II SS Panzer Corps comprising units from the 3rd *Volksgrenadier* Division were attacking Elsenborn. Artillery and rocket-launcher fire from the 12th *Volksgrenadier* Division attacked Hünningen, Mürringen and Büllingen. The 1st SS Panzer Corps recaptured Stavelot, while the 9th SS Panzer Division was advancing on Vielsalm with the 3rd Panzergrenadier Division taking Krinkelt, but had encountered strong enemy resistance during the attack on Bütgenbach village. To support this attack, the 12th SS *Hitlerjugend* reported that its units were ready to advance on the estate. However, marshy sections and extensive forests prevented heavy armour from being put into action in the area and it was left to *Volksgrenadiers* and SS soldiers to capture on foot.

However, the following day, the 12th SS was still fighting for Bütgenbach together with the 12th *Volksgrenadier* Division. Stiff enemy pressure prevented units from capturing the village and continuing their march. An armoured group was then called into action comprising the Panzer Regiment of I *Abteilung* and *Schwere Panzerjäger Abteilung* 12, both of which only had small numbers of panzers and *Panzerjägers* which had to wheel through the thick boggy mud. The attack on the village was limited, but according to reports a Panther of *SS-Sturmbannführer* Arnold Jurgensen was put out of action as he and one of his crew were seriously burned.

In spite of the losses the attack continued, but SS strength had been severely weakened by enemy artillery fire and tank destroyers. With the lack of additional support, commanders in the field considered pulling out the SS in the area, but instead decided to use the 12th SS to concentrate its efforts on keeping the road to Malmedy open instead.

Elsewhere along the front, the situation in some sectors for the Germans was showing signs of deterioration. The right wing of the 6th Panzer Army, for instance, was stalled with its units trying to establish contact with the far advanced *Kampfgruppe Peiper* in order to gain momentum and re-start the attack. In other areas, however, there were still successes. The 5th Panzer Army with its flanks covered by the 6th Panzer Army and 7th Army achieved major success. It was able to take full advantage of the dense network of roads with a number of good routes of advance along the Maas river line. Other units such as the 18th *Volksgrenadier* Division managed to capture a strategic road traffic centre of St. Vith against the US 7th Armoured Division.

In other sectors, the 2nd Panzer Division pushed past the town of Bastogne to the north. The 2nd SS Panzer Division *Das Reich* and the 9th SS *Hohenstaufen* were moving well and driving back the enemy. The men of the *Hohenstaufen* Division attacked the Salm sector near Grand-Halleux. The *Das Reich* Division captured Salmchâteau, while *Kampfgruppe der Führer* raced some 10 miles west, reached the village of Baraque de Fraiture and attacked it.

Further along the front the *SS-Leibstandarte* were struggling to break through to *Kampfgruppe Peiper*, who had now become encircled in La Gleize, and establish contact. The I SS Panzer Corps ordered the *Kampfgruppe* to break out. Already the important towns of Stoumont and Cheneux had to be given up. By Christmas morning the *Kampfgruppe* succeeded in reaching the German lines south-west of Wanne on foot. They had left behind 250 American prisoners as well as 200 wounded Germans and Americans. The *Kampfgruppe* had managed to pull out some 800 troops, but 35 panzers, 60 armoured personnel carriers and 2 artillery batteries all had to be reluctantly left behind.

Meanwhile, further south, about an hour's drive from La Gleize, developments had been building around the town of Bastogne on the River Meuse. Manteuffel's 5th Panzer Army had pushed forward under the cover of fog, advancing towards the town of Bastogne. En route, in the town of Clervaux soldiers of the 2nd Panzer Division fought a series of close-quarter battles in which both sides incurred losses. However, despite desperate attempts by the Americans to beat off the attack, they were unable to neutralize the strength of the Germans and were consequently driven out or captured. After a few hours, the town finally fell, leaving the way open for the Germans to advance on Bastogne.

(**Opposite, above**) A photograph from a still film showing Model conferring with an *SS-Unterscharführer* during the early phase of the Ardennes offensive. Model was commander of Army Group B, which contained four armies. Although the 15th Army was not to take part in the operations, the 6th Panzer Army, 5th Panzer Army and 7th Army were all to play a decisive role. All three armies were to attack the American positions between Monschau in the north and Echternach in the south.

(**Opposite, below**) Commanders confer with the aid of a map during the opening phase of the Ardennes offensive. Behind them is a column of Sd.Kfz.251 armoured half-track personnel carriers, which are preparing to move forward into action.

A *Fallschirmjäger* mortar crew plug their ears as the projectile from an 8cm sGrW 34 mortar can be seen leaving the gun tube. It was very common for infantry, especially during long intensive periods of action, to fire their mortar either from trenches or dug-in positions where the mortar crew could also be protected from enemy fire.

An 8.8cm FlaK gun fires at an enemy position. The gun's high velocity and flat trajectory made it very accurate and effective in both the anti-aircraft and anti-tank role. Note the gun's limber positioned nearby. The limber was normally positioned like this in order for the crew to rapidly limber up and reposition the gun.

A tank commander signals his unit to move forward into action by waving his arm.

Two photographs showing the gun crew of a 2cm FlaK 38 preparing the gun for action in the field.

Two photographs showing the 2cm FlaK 38 being readied for a fire mission against an enemy target. This weapon was the most numerously-produced German artillery piece utilized by the Wehrmacht, Luftwaffe and the Waffen-SS. This particular gun is mounted on an Sd.Ah.52 trailer and could be towed behind a variety of half-tracks.

Three photographs taken in sequence showing SS Panzergrenadiers moving forward into action supported by an Sd.Kfz.251 half-track, which mounts an MG 42 machine gun for local defence. These front-wheel-steering vehicles with tracked drive transformed the fighting ability of both the Wehrmacht and Waffen-SS throughout the war. They were used extensively in the Ardennes, not only to carry troops into battle but also to tow ordnance and stow other important equipment.

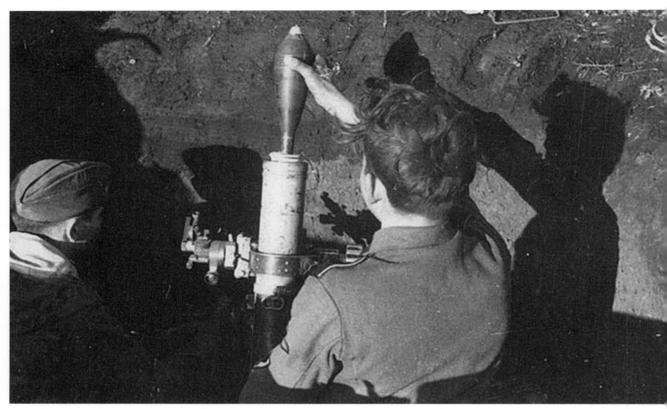

A mortar crew can be seen in a standard dugout loading a projectile during a preliminary fire mission against an enemy position.

A still from a German propaganda film showing *SS-Obersturmführer* Joachim Peiper with a map conferring with one of his staff officers. Peiper's *Kampfgruppe*, comprising the most substantial armoured group within the SS *Leibstandarte*, contained the powerful 501st Heavy Panzer Battalion of King Tigers.

Grenadiers being transported into battle by an Sd.Kfz.251 half-track. Note the splinter shield and the mounted MG 42 machine gun for local defence. All the soldiers have foliage attached to their steel helmets.

A photo of *SS-Obersturmführer* Joachim Peiper. Although Peiper was a brilliant armoured strategist, he was also a callous and ruthless commander in the field. At a crossroads at Baugnez near Malmedy, along the advancing northern wing of Peiper's *Kampfgruppe*, approximately 125 soldiers of Battery B of the American 285th Field Artillery Observation Battalion were captured and herded into an open field. Hanstholm Siptrott, the commander of Panzer 731, was then ordered to open fire on the prisoners, murdering them.

(**Above**) A late-variant Pz.Kpfw.IV belonging to *Kampfgruppe Peiper* advances along a road following a number of successful engagements against the enemy. The sudden speed and depth of the German attack through the Ardennes was quick and decisive. US troops were totally caught off guard by the enormity of the attack. As a result, hundreds of American soldiers were captured along the front lines. In this photograph, although not clear, are US PoWs sitting on an embankment watching Peiper's tanks roll past.

(**Opposite, above**) A *Sturmgeschütz* III Ausf.G rolls into action. A crew member waves to the photographer. This assault gun is armed with the punchy 7.5cm StuK 40 L/48 gun which is housed in a cast *Topfblende* (pot-mantlet). Note the two kill rings painted around the gun tube, near the double-baffle muzzle brake. These assault guns were initially put into the field to operate in close support of the infantry, following behind the advancing troops and providing high-explosive artillery fire in order to help overcome any enemy strongpoints that were holding up the advance. However, by 1944, because of the lack of tanks in the dwindling ranks of the panzer divisions, the StuG III was used alongside the panzer until the end of the war, more as an anti-tank weapon rather than supporting the infantry, which had been its intended role.

(**Opposite, below**) A well-concealed FlaK gun hidden among the undergrowth inside a forest.

(**Above**) SS troops moving forward into action. These soldiers appear to be part of an MG 42 machine-gun crew.

(**Opposite, above**) SS soldiers have hitched a lift onboard a tank bound for the front lines.

(**Opposite, below**) A StuG IV churns along a muddy road. This late-production assault gun comprised single 80mm-thick armour plate on the starboard-side casemate front. Attached to the roof is a 360-degree mounted traverse MG 42 for close defence. Note half of the vehicle's side skirts or Schürzen are missing and saplings can be seen attached to parts of the side armour.

Two Waffen-SS Volkswagen *Schwimmwagen* amphibious vehicles wade across one of the many streams and rivers that cut through the Ardennes.

A grenadier looks at his new hand-held *Panzerfaust* while his comrades in the field also take some interest in this lethal anti-tank weapon. By this period of the war, at regimental level an anti-tank company comprised a platoon equipped with three PaK guns and two platoons armed with *Panzerfausts*. A number of units operating in the Ardennes were made up of recruits that had little training, many of them not even having held a rifle before. Nevertheless, these soldiers were given light anti-tank weapons mainly comprising *Panzerfausts* and were put in line to knock out enemy armour.

(**Above**) Waffen-SS troops on board a *Jagdpanzer* IV. Note one soldier is standing on the damaged side skirt and shouting orders. The *Jagdpanzer* IV armed with its 7.5cm PaK 39 L/48 cannon was a very effective panzer-hunter in the Ardennes and scored considerable successes during a number of actions. However, like many of the vehicles that entered service during the latter stages of the war, they were too few or too dispersed to do little but temporarily achieve a number of successes.

(**Opposite, above**) A commanding officer converses with his men.

(**Opposite, below**) A reconnaissance position and a radio crew can be seen in a slit trench.

A King Tiger tank rolls along a road followed by two motorcyclists armed with the MP 40 machine pistol slung around their back for ease of carriage. Moving in the opposite direction is a column of American troops captured during the initial stages of the Ardennes offensive.

A winter-clad SS soldier can be seen in a slit trench, which were dug extensively in the Ardennes.

The first of two photographs, of different quality, taken in sequence showing *SS-Sturmbannführer* Josef Diefenthal watching American troops belonging to the US 119th Infantry Regiment of the 30th Infantry Division surrender on 19 December in Stoumont, Belgium. Though a cold-blooded commander who had committed war crimes in the Ardennes, Diefenthal went on to receive the Knight's Cross of the Iron Cross for his actions in the Ardennes while in command of the 3rd Battalion, 2nd SS Panzergrenadier Regiment of the SS *Leibstandarte*. His unit was known in the field as *Kampfgruppe Diefenthal*.

(**Opposite, above**) A Waffen-SS StuG IV moves across an open field passing captured American vehicles. Typical of this variant, the assault gun mounts its StuK 40 inside a cast pot-mantlet or *Topfblende*. Note the extensive use of zimmerit anti-magnetic mine paste applied over the armoured plates of the vehicle. The near-side track guard appears to have been damaged and is buckled upwards.

(**Opposite, below**) Grenadiers make a dash across a snowy field armed with their Karabiner 98k bolt-action rifles.

(**Opposite, above**) Grenadiers from *Kampfgruppe Peiper* can be seen in the town of Honsfeld surveying American equipment left behind by the 394th Regiment of the US 99th Infantry Division. The town of Honsfeld had been a rest area for the American regiment. Fearing they would be cut off and destroyed by Peiper's advancing forces, many soldiers began fleeing the town. Within hours of the first bombardments, Peiper's Panthers moved into its streets and captured it.

(**Opposite, below**) A column of captured American soldiers are led along a road.

(**Above**) A Tiger II on the advance passes a long column of captured American soldiers that are being escorted to the rear.

A grenadier armed with his Karabiner bolt-action rifle can be seen moving quickly along the side of a road which is littered with abandoned and knocked-out US army vehicles.

Chapter Three

Race for Bastogne

The town of Bastogne was the headquarters of the American VIII Corps commanded by General Middleton. Being the centre of the road network on the German line of advance, the Americans became quickly aware that the town could be held, and then the chances of success for the Germans reaching the River Meuse would be seriously disrupted. Middleton called for every man available to defend the town. Clerks, cooks, headquarters staff and soldiers, who had never fought, were quickly given training in how to fire a bazooka, a trench mortar or to set a mine. Anti-tank, anti-aircraft guns and roadblocks were employed to form a defensive screen erected along a 7- to 8-mile-long arc between Bastogne and the villages of Foy and Neffe. The 82nd and the 101st Airborne divisions were the only real defence of Bastogne and were ordered from Reims 100 miles away to help defend the town. From the opposite direction, the Germans were also advancing on the town at breakneck speed. To them, the capture of Bastogne was not a symbolic one, it was essential to the development of their offensive through Belgium. Leading the German advance to Bastogne in his armoured half-track was divisional commander General Fritz Bayerlein, followed by the 901st Panzergrenadier Regiment of the Panzer Lehr Division. Their drive on the town was hampered by bad roads and through the village of Margaret where its units stumbled onto a hospital unit, which it then captured. The division then swung round to its rear and attacked an American column that had earlier passed through the town. What followed was a number of panzers exposing American troops to a murderous concentration of fire. Nothing, it seemed, was able to withstand this German armoured onslaught. In the confusion and mayhem that followed, American troops abandoned their vehicles, trying in vain to scramble away. However, the tanks were fast and driven by fearless crews and before some had the chance to escape, the Germans, showing no mercy, tore them to shreds. A German tank commander wrote:

> Even myself, a veteran of the Eastern Front, was shocked by the destruction. The dead lined the ditches and mud tracks, while further up the road an armada of American vehicles had fallen victim to our attack. At first, our enemy had put up no resistance, and most of its sad remnants were scattered along the road towards Bastogne.

Nearly 200 American vehicles had been destroyed, but despite losses in men and matériel, the Germans had paid a high price. It had resulted in delaying the division arriving in Bastogne by a day, by which time the 101st had reached the town.

During the night of 18/19 December, two German panzer divisions arrived at the edge of Bastogne. Throughout the 19th, fighting raged around the town along the exit roads and inside the surrounding villages. Around Bastogne, Sherman tanks acted as a mobile striking force, ready to plug any breach at a moment's notice. Dawn on the 20th found the perimeter still intact and revealed two destroyed panzers at its edge, but the town was almost completely surrounded. For the next twenty-four hours, only isolated pockets of fighting occurred around the town. While American stocks of ammunition continued to dwindle, the Germans were bringing up substantial reinforcements. General Brandenberger's 7th Army promised General Heinrich Lüttwitz, commander of the elite XLVIII Panzer, that the 5th *Fallschirmjäger* Division was on its way to join his troops at Bastogne. By dawn on 22 December, elements of that division arrived ready for action. Later that day, while German armoured units were poised to attack the town in considerable strength, a four-man German party under a white flag came forward to the American lines on the Arlon highway wishing to speak to the American general commanding Bastogne. *Oberleutnant* Helmuth Henke of Panzer Lehr's operations section spoke English and asked a group of American troops to carry their demand to their commander for 'the honourable surrender of the town'. The surrender note was in turn passed to General McAuliffe, who disdainfully replied in a message to the German commander: 'Nuts!' Henke was not sure what the reply meant. He was told in plain English by Colonel Harper commanding the 327th that it is the same thing as 'Go to hell!' Harper went on and told Henke that 'if you continue to attack, we will kill every goddamn German who tries to break this city!' Henke saluted and replied: 'We will kill many Americans. This is war.' The German party returned to their lines.

By now it became clear to German commanders in the field that the American Bastogne salient posed such a threat to the flank and rear of German Army Group B that the battle could no longer be ignored. In fact, Bastogne was becoming the centre of gravity of the whole battle in the Ardennes.

After almost a week of bad weather, 23 December dawned clear and cold. For the beleaguered Americans at Bastogne, this was a relief as they now expected air-drops of supplies from flights of bombers. During the afternoon, 241 transport planes dropped loads totalling 144 tons of supplies over the town. A number of planes were shot down or forced to turn back because of heavy German anti-aircraft fire, but generally most of the parachute packs, which weighed 1,200lb apiece, fell inside the American perimeter. P-47 fighters escorting the transports turned and attacked the German positions around the town and struck their lines hard. In turn, the Germans mounted a series of heavy multi-pronged attacks against the American perimeter.

In preparation for operations in the snow, a great majority of Germans had hurriedly painted their vehicles white and their infantrymen were dressed in white snow-camouflage smocks. The Americans had also hastily whitewashed their tanks and tank-destroyers, half-tracks and jeeps, and a number of American soldiers took bed linen from local civilians for conversion into snow smocks. For a number of hours, the fighting see-sawed with the Germans renewing their assaults with great energy and determination including heavy artillery bombing of the town. Both sides incurred huge losses, but still the Americans were resolute in defending the town and preventing its loss. Whole areas, including the town square, were badly hit.

On Christmas Day the fighting continued with unabated ferocity. Around the smouldering town American tanks, half-tracks and advancing infantry moved into action. German grenadiers and American armoured infantry became locked in a desperate battle of attrition. Although the German grenadiers displayed skill and tenacity, the resolute Americans made a number of successful penetrating strikes, causing considerable damage to their foe. An exhausted German soldier said:

> I was completely shocked by the resistance the Americans had shown. We had been told that these men were badly trained and were not real soldiers. It soon became apparent how wrong this was. Constantly we met savage engagements, some of them hand-to-hand. The loss of men was terrible.

Slowly and inexorably, Patton's 4th Armoured Division broke through the ring to help relieve the encircled Bastogne. Yet despite the terrible casualties, the Germans remained strong, determined more than ever to capture the town, whatever the cost. In a last desperate effort to smash their way through, an elite *Kampfgruppe* was formed out of the wreckage of the *SS-Leibstandarte* brought down from the 6th SS Panzer Army's front and a division of infantry specially transported from Hungary, the 167th *Volksgrenadiers*, most of which were ex-veterans recently bloodied from the Eastern Front. Headquarters Army Group B reported on 28 December: '*Kampfgruppe* 1st SS Panzer Division, with its Panzer Regiment, *Panzer-jäger* Battalion, 1st Panzergrenadier Regiment, Artillery Regiment, Pioneer Company and Armoured Reconnaissance Platoon left the Vielsalm area at 1625 hours and moved into the … Longvilly area.'

At dawn on 30 December, the attack began with lightning strikes utilizing the main armour of the Waffen-SS, notably those from units of the *Leibstandarte* comprising Panthers and Pz.Kpfw.IVs. Supporting these tanks were Karl Rettlinger's 1st SS *Panzerjäger* Battalion, which had suffered little and comprised some eighteen *Jagdpanzer* IVs along with the corps' 501st SS Heavy Battalion. How many of these tanks and *Jagdpanzer* actually reached the Bastogne area is uncertain, but out of a total of ninety-three, it is unlikely that more than fifty saw action in the area. With regard to infantry, Hansen's 2nd and Rudolf Sandig's 1st SS Panzergrenadier battalions were allocated to *Kampfgruppe Poetschke*, while Hansen was left with the remnants of his 1st and 3rd battalions. Overall, the *Leibstandarte Kampfgruppe* that was rushed to Bastogne probably had the equivalent of about one panzergrenadier battalion.

With this armour, and support from the 12 SS *Hitlerjugend*, *Fallschirmjäger* and *Volksgrenadier*, fierce, confused fighting raged with Americans calling in tanks, fighter-bombers and heavy artillery support. During the battle, the *Leibstandarte* lost thirty panzers with soldiers taking a severe hammering. A *Fallschirmjäger* trooper noted:

> The enemy had offered the most bitter resistance and employed masses of artillery and armour. We consequently suffered heavy losses. Above us fighter-bombers and artillery-spotting aircraft clouded the sky without opposition. They swooped down and attacked any vehicle or movement on the roads and open fields. In the confusion, some of us took cover behind a lonely house where they discovered some jarred men of the elite *SS-Leibstandarte* were sheltering.

On 2 January, the chief command of I.SS Panzer Corps submitted a planned attack around Bastogne to the 5th Panzer Army. The 26th *Volksgrenadier* Division was to attack from the west of the Houffalize-Bastogne road, the 340th *Volksgrenadier* Division along both sides of the railway line between Bourcy and Bastogne, and the 12 SS *Hitlerjugend* from the area around Michamps on Bastogne. Supporting this drive was the 9 SS Panzer Division. The attack was scheduled to commence on 3 January.

The attack opened up with a heavy artillery barrage against American defensive positions holding the perimeter of the town. The *Hohenstaufen* Division attacked with Panzergrenadier Regiment 19 and Panzergrenadier Regiment 9, which had thirty operational panzers. Panzergrenadier Regiment 20 arrived later and joined the attack.

The attack went well, with Supreme Command West noting: 'Our assault troops mounted an attack on Bastogne from the north and north-east. They were able to gain much ground against bitter enemy resistance. The wood north-east of Bizory was reached. Margaret was captured. The battles are continuing.'

By 7 January the 12 SS *Hitlerjugend* had brought its spearheads to the railway station within 2 miles of the centre of Bastogne. However, losses were considerable. Snow and ice was also a hindrance and fuel was desperately required. Heavy resistance by the Americans also played a crucial part in operations to defend Bastogne.

Over the following days the weather became even more appalling, with temperatures around zero. The fighting around the town had become so bad that some battalions incurred 40 per cent casualties. Even General Patterson remarked in his diary: 'We can still lose this war.' Yet slowly, with additional support from the British XXX Corps, the Germans were forced on the defensive and driven back, this time for good. Almost 12,000 German soldiers were killed attempting to capture Bastogne and 900 Americans died defending it, with another 3,000 killed outside its perimeter. From the pulverizing effects of ground and air attacks, the Germans had left behind 450 tanks and armoured vehicles, with the Americans losing 150 tanks and vehicles.

StuG IIIs advance along a road bound for the front. The leading vehicle still retains its summer camouflage scheme.

SS grenadiers during a pause in their advance on their way to Bastogne. One of the soldiers has a *Panzerfaust* slung over his shoulder, while his comrade is drinking a Belgian beer.

(**Opposite, above**) An Sd.Kfz.251 half-track of *Kampfgruppe Peiper* has pulled into a captured village in southern Belgium. Note the SS grenadiers surveying an abandoned American half-track.

(**Opposite, below**) A grenadier is about to climb into an Sd.Kfz.251 half-track. These personnel carriers were used extensively throughout the war and were one of the most popular armoured vehicles used by the Waffen-SS in the Ardennes.

(**Above**) A grenadier pauses in his march, smoking a cigarette. He wears the standard army greatcoat and a black woollen toque to keep him warm.

An SS officer makes a note in his writing pad against a tree inside a forest.

A variety of armoured vehicles comprising a Pz.Kpfw.IV, Sd.Kfz.251 half-tracks, support vehicles and a light Horch cross-country vehicle roll through a Belgian village.

A soldier wearing his distinctive SS anorak pauses during his march for a cigarette.

An injured soldier is being helped by two of his comrades. They are all wearing the winter reversibles white-side-out.

A young SS grenadier in a foxhole smiles for the camera beneath the hood of his fur-lined anorak.

A photograph showing SS winter-clad soldiers pausing in the fighting for a cigarette.

(**Opposite, above**) Two Sd.Kfz.251s, one an Ausf.C and the other an Ausf.D, pull alongside each other. The crews appear to be exchanging details. The Ausf.C mounts the typical frame antenna, while the Ausf.D has no antenna. Both mount the MG 34 machine gun with splinter shield.

(**Opposite, below**) Whitewashed self-propelled Wespes can be seen advancing across the snowy terrain bound for the front. The vehicles were allocated to the armoured artillery battalions (*Panzer-Artillerie Abteilungen*) of panzer divisions and brought greater mobility to the artillery formations of the panzer divisions.

(**Above**) In the Ardennes and a Pz.Kpfw.IV has been concealed by the crew with wooden planks, foliage and branches from the surrounding trees. The Panzer is further concealed parked next to a derelict building.

(**Above**) During their advance on the town of Bastogne, SS troops have retrieved an injured comrade and are moving him by sled to a field hospital.

(**Opposite**) Obviously working in very cold conditions, the loader rams home a complete projectile in the FlaK 8.8cm gun. Note the shield forward of the pneumatic recuperator; the small cylinder on top of it is a cover for the mount for an indirect-fire RB1f sight which was used when the gun was deployed in a conventional field artillery role.

(**Below**) A FlaK 8.8cm gun positioned in the snow during a lull in the fighting.

Here a crewman prepares to launch his *Panzerwerfer 42 auf Maultier*, Sd.Kfz.4/1. He is standing on the open hatches through which rockets are being passed. Note a jerry can wedged behind the forward wheels to help keep the vehicle from moving when the rockets were fired. The back-blast from the *Nebelwerfer* was very powerful and could often move a vehicle as large as this by 12 inches.

Heavily supplied infantry supporting the SS can be seen advancing at speed across a field. (*NARA*)

Two photographs taken in sequence showing the *Panzerwerfer 42 auf Maultier*, Sd.Kfz.4/1 being prepared for action against enemy positions. This weapon was used for larger-scale rocket barrages against enemy positions where a large bombardment of a big area would be more effective than artillery fire. In the Ardennes and against the town of Bastogne these weapons saw intensive use and were concentrated in massed salvos, causing considerable damage and losses in men and matériel. (*NARA*)

Three photographs taken in sequence showing a *Nebelwefer* brigade preparing and firing against enemy positions. When fired the projectiles screamed through the air, causing the enemy to become unnerved by the noise. Initially these fearsome weapons served in independent army rocket-launcher battalions and by 1945 they operated in regiments and brigades. They were used extensively in the Ardennes and were one of the main weapons used in the initial attack. In fact, 340 *Nebelwerfers* were directed against American positions between Höfen and the Losheim Gap. The sound of these thundering across the sky must have been terrifying.

An SS crew of an Sd.Kfz.251/10 can be seen during their advance across a snowy field in early January 1945.

A smiling SS officer watches his comrade drink a bottle of beer inside an Sd.Kfz.251/3 *Mittlerer Kommandopanzerwagen* (*Funkpanzerwagen*) communication vehicle.

A Maultier truck more than likely carrying supplies can be seen here on a road bound for Bastogne. An 8.8cm FlaK crew is guarding the stretch of road against possible ground or aerial enemy attacks.

More than likely in a forward observation post and this SS artillery or FlaK observer can be seen with his Zeiss 12 × 60 range-finder trying to calculate the location and distance of the enemy.

A PaK crew preparing their antiquated PaK 35/36 anti-tank gun. Although these weapons had more or less been relegated to training purposes, both the Wehrmacht and Waffen-SS still used them on the battlefield as they were light and versatile, especially in the snow.

A camouflaged 8.8cm FlaK gun can be seen here with its barrel elevated horizontally, indicating it being utilized in a ground-attack role. Crew members are surveying the snowy terrain ahead for possible movements of the enemy.

Grenadiers on a road bound for Bastogne. Behind them, buildings are seen burning. By early January units of the 12 SS *Hitlerjugend* were reported to be within 2 miles of the centre of Bastogne. However, losses were considerable due to strong American resistance in defending the town.

Surveying enemy positions and a winter-clad SS grenadier can be seen looking through 6 × 30 Zeiss binoculars.

(**Above**) A photograph taken from inside a house looking out through a window showing SS soldiers who appear to be cutting wood for a fire.

(**Opposite, above**) The crew of a whitewashed Pz.Kpfw.IV.

(**Opposite, below**) A commander inside an Sd.Kfz.251 Ausf.C is conferring with a soldier. The Ausf.C has the typical frame antenna and mounts the MG 42 machine gun with splinter shield.

Two SS grenadiers are seen here conversing and smiling while smoking a cigarette. They both wear the reversible winter jacket but grey-side-out.

SS soldiers march along an icy road in the snow. Weather conditions by early January 1945 were miserable for both sides, and in some areas movement was hindered by heavy snow and the lack of tracked vehicles.

A wounded German soldier is being carried on a stretcher. Nearly 12,000 German soldiers were killed attempting to capture Bastogne and 900 Americans died defending it, with another 3,000 killed outside its perimeter.

Chapter Four

Turning-Point

All over the Ardennes, German soldiers were exhausted. For days and nights, in the wet and cold, they pushed westwards towards a promised victory. Nourished by their early success and apparent lack of resistance, their forces began to wither as stores of rations, lack of sleep and the constant shelling and bombing from aerial attack drained their energy. Major General Richard Metz, the commander of the 5th Panzer Army's artillery, declared: 'The attacks from the air were so powerful that evening a single vehicle could only get through by going from cover to cover.' Constantly, German soldiers threw themselves into ditches or dugouts, helpless against the mighty Allied Air Force. In just four days, from when the Allied air offensive was unleashed on 23 December, 7,000 sorties were flown and many critical points were hit on the Ardennes battlefield. Wave after wave of aircraft systematically pounded German lines of communication all the way back to the Rhine. As a result, the Ardennes offensive slowly ground to a halt. With the German armoured spearheads bedevilled by broken lines of communication and lack of fuel, the Allies were given a breathing space to create a firm defensive line and make plans for their own advance east. Some commanders, however, like Model and Manteuffel, were not discouraged by the state of the offensive. They believed, as long as Bastogne could be captured, Patton's counterattack held and fresh battleworthy units could be rushed up to the front in time, there was no reason why certain limited objectives of the offensive could not be achieved.

However, all over the German front fighting began to get harder and resistance was difficult to overcome. Even the most irrepressible Waffen-SS soldiers were constantly finding themselves beaten back and sustaining terrible costs in men and matériel. Even Hitler's drastic attempts to release from reserve 9th SS Panzer Division and 15th Panzergrenadier Division to reinforce Manteuffel's army to hold the town of Celles, just 5 miles from the Meuse, failed due to the relentless push of VII Corps, commanded by General Collins, nicknamed 'Lightning Joe' by his men. This German failure marked the turning-point of the offensive.

Along the entire front German soldiers were becoming increasingly exhausted and worn down. In a drastic attempt to assist the failing drive to the River Meuse, additional troops were thrown in to launch a new offensive in Alsace, where the

Americans had drained their forces in order to send reinforcements north into the Ardennes. The code-name was *Nordwind* and it was launched in earnest on New Year's Day with eight divisions spearheaded by an SS Korps consisting of the 17th SS Panzergrenadier Division *Götz von Berlichingen* and the 36th *Volksgrenadier* Division. At first the offensive went relatively well, but heavy resistance soon forced the Germans back. The subsequent commitment of the 10th SS Panzer Division *Frundsberg* and the 6th SS *Gebirgs-Division Nord* failed to alter the situation in the area.

With so many Allied forces being employed in the Ardennes, it slowly forced Hitler to realize how dangerous the war in the West had become. During the first days of January 1945, the weather became even more appalling, with temperatures falling to around zero.

On 8 January, with more than 100,000 Germans dead on the battlefield, the Führer grudgingly ordered the remnants of forward units to fall back to a line running south from Dochamps in the Samrée-Baraque de Fraiture area to Longchamp, 5 miles north of Bastogne. Even more significant were orders for the mighty elite SS Panzer divisions to go over to the defensive. The 6th SS Panzer Army was withdrawn into reserve under Hitler's personal command and he also called back remnants of his foremost fighting machine – the *Leibstandarte* – from the Bastogne area. Panzers coming off the assembly lines were diverted from the Ardennes back to the Eastern Front, and there were no more propaganda broadcasts in Germany about the 'historic offensive'. Field Marshal von Rundstedt, who claimed that the Ardennes offensive was 'Stalingrad No. 2', was so sickened by the death and destruction in Belgium that he informed his weary commanders that there was now no more prospect for success. The end had finally come and Hitler had lost his last gamble in the West forever.

(**Opposite, above**) A battery of SiG33 howitzers being used against American positions. These weapons were the standard German heavy infantry gun used throughout the war. It was the largest classified infantry gun used by both the Wehrmacht and Waffen-SS.

(**Opposite, below**) Various armoured vehicles including two Pz.Kpfw.IVs and half-tracks supporting an advance through a wooded area in Belgium. Utilizing a number of half-tracks was the most effective and quickest way of being transported either to the battlefield or being withdrawn to another line of defence. When the half-tracks arrived at the edge of a battlefield, the troops were able to quickly dismount to take up positions.

Three photographs taken in sequence showing a Panther V Ausf.G rolling along a snowy road during the Ardennes operation in late 1944. Panthers made up the bulk of the armoured strength with seven panzer divisions assigned to the offensive. *Kampfgruppe Peiper* was the main spearheading force and made its furthest advance at Stoumont, far from the River Meuse, their objective. After securing an American fuel dump at Büllingen and bypassing American strongpoints at Elsenborn Ridge, *Kampfgruppe Peiper* advanced through Stavelot and Baugnez, but American engineers blew bridges as they approached Trois-Points. Peiper decided to halt his armour for fuel supplies and reinforcements at La Gleize, with a small reinforced reconnaissance to Stoumont. However, beaten back, his *Kampfgruppe* held La Gleize against the growing might of American forces, which fought bitterly to recapture the town. Peiper soon became encircled. The I SS Panzer Korps ordered the *Kampfgruppe* to break out. By Christmas morning they succeeded in breaking out and reaching the German lines south-west of Wanne on foot. They had left behind thirty-five panzers, sixty armoured personnel carriers and two artillery batteries.

A Panzer crew converses with a commanding officer in thick snow during operations in late December 1944. By the end of December 1944 the whole position in the Ardennes was on the point of disintegration for the Germans. Fighting had been a gruelling battle of attrition for both German and Allied units.

SS riflemen armed with the Karabiner 98k bolt-action rifle can be seen sharing a cigarette.

From his cupola a Panzer commander reaches out and greets a Wehrmacht grenadier in a snowy field.

Two photographs of a grenadier armed with the deadly *Panzerfaust*. During the last year of the war the *Panzerfaust* was used extensively to combat enemy armour. It was a hand-held rocket-propelled grenade, which was effective at a range of about 90ft. By early 1945, there was a dramatic increase in the loss of Allied tanks to the *Panzerfaust* and more than half of the tanks knocked out in combat were destroyed by the *Panzerfaust* or *Panzerschreck*.

A blurred photograph showing winter-clad SS assisting and recovering an injured comrade from the battlefield.

Two commanders converse from inside what appears to be a half-track and discuss with other officers strategic plans with the aid of a map. From the appearance of their faces, the weather is very cold. In fact, during the first days of January 1945, the weather had further deteriorated with daytime temperatures falling below zero.

Standing up here in his cupola is a Waffen-SS tank commander wearing his panzer headphones. These headphones had a dual-purpose role: radio communication with other armoured vehicles and communication with other members of the vehicle's crew. These headphones were often used in conjunction with the throat-microphone set. (*NARA*)

This Sd.Kfz.251 appears to have attempted to conceal itself in undergrowth and become stuck when the crew decided to move it out of concealment. A number of SS grenadiers have attempted to assist in pushing this half-track through the snow. Note four jerry cans attached to the side of the vehicle. By this period of the campaign fuel was at a premium and a number of vehicles were already running out of fuel and being abandoned by their crews.

A half-track belonging to the 116th Panzer Division, known as the *Windhund* (Greyhound) Division. Just prior to the Ardennes offensive, on 10 December the division was partly refitted with twenty-six Pz.Kpfw.IVs, forty-three Panthers and twenty-five *Jagdpanzer* IV tank destroyers. It was deemed a very powerful panzer division; however, it still lacked sufficient supplies when it attacked American positions. In spite of this, it became heavily embroiled in the fighting and fought its way towards the Meuse supporting Waffen-SS units. It then saw extensive action at Hotton and Verdenne, but due to heavy losses and outstripping its remaining supplies it turned back at its furthest advance in the Ardennes.

During the campaign in the Ardennes, especially when the area received extensive snow by late December, German troops were able to adapt their reversible winter wear from grey-side to white-side-out. This photograph shows an SS soldier in his winter white reversibles. Note how dirty they have become, which often made concealment in the snow more difficult.

A whitewashed late-variant Pz.Kpfw.IV with intact *Schürzen* is being guided through a forest by one of its crew members. Sitting on board the engine deck hitching a lift are a number of winter-clad SS grenadiers.

As the evening begins to draw in, an injured SS soldier is being assisted to safety by his comrades. By early January 1945, losses in German troops killed and injured were mounting, causing parts of the front to cave in or become inactive. Moving in daylight had also become a serious concern and with no Luftwaffe cover, men and armour were now constantly exposed to the full brutal force of Allied air attacks.

Oberleutnant Eberhard Lemor of the 217th *Sturmpanzer Abteilung* 217 with his *Brummbär* in the Ardennes in January 1945. Note he is aided by a crutch as he wears a recently-applied plaster cast over his broken left leg. Behind him sits his *Sturmpanzer* IV.

Men from *Sturmpanzer Abteilung* 217 during a reconnaissance operation.

Three photographs taken in sequence showing a *Sturmpanzer* IV *Brummbär* negotiating the uneven terrain in the Ardennes. This vehicle was attached to *Sturmpanzer Abteilung* 217. On 19 December with thirty-one vehicles *Abteilung* 217 only managed to advance as far as St. Vith before it was halted by strong enemy resistance. In early January the battalion was forced to withdraw.

(**Above**) *Oberleutnant* Eberhard Lemor of the 217th *Sturmpanzer Abteilung* 217 confers with his commanders in the field in early January 1945.

(**Opposite, above**) Winter-clad grenadiers smile for the camera on board a *Sturmgeschütz* III during the early phase of Operation NORDWIND. By the later part of December 1944, with the German momentum during the Ardennes offensive beginning to dissipate, it became evident that the operation was on the verge of collapse. German tacticians therefore decided that in order to relieve the pressure on forces in the Ardennes they would attack the US Seventh Army in southern France. The operation was an offensive to break through the lines of the US Seventh Army and French 1st Army in the Upper Vosges Mountains and surround and destroy the enemy forces. However, despite an audacious start to the German offensive, they were not able to avert the situation and destroy the American forces. By the time the operation came to an end, the Ardennes offensive had already been called off by Hitler.

(**Opposite, below**) A PaK gunner lies dead, sprawled out in a field next to his destroyed PaK gun.

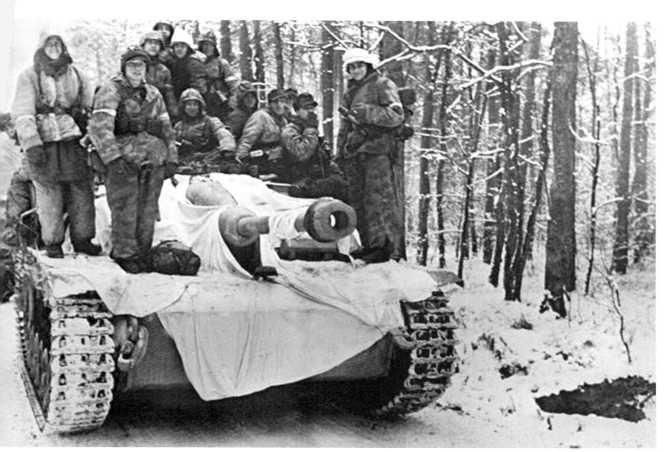

A German unit carries a wounded soldier on a stretcher to a field hospital in early January 1945. They pass a camouflaged stationary Sd.Kfz.251 half-track.

Two young *Hitlerjugend* soldiers captured in Belgium in early January 1945. Both of these boys were part of the 12th SS Panzer Division *Hitlerjugend*. (NARA)

Appendix

Waffen-SS Order of Battle

Ardennes, December 1944–January 1945

Heeresgruppe B

Generalfeldmarschall Walther Model
Chef: *General der Infanterie* Hans Krebs
SS-Sturmbannführer Heinrich Springer, aide-de-camp to *Generalfeldmarschall* Model
Units:
III.*FlaK Korps*: *Generalleutnant* Wolfgang Pickert (2 Aug. 1944–20 Mar. 1945)
813 Panzer *Pionier-Kompanie*
725 *Eisenbahn (RR) Artillerie-Abteilung*
674 *Eisenbahn-Artillerie-Batterie*
688 *Eisenbahn-Artillerie-Batterie*
749 *Eisenbahn-Artillerie-Batterie*

OKW Reserve

79 *Volksgrenadier* Division: *Generalmajor* Alois Weber
257 *Volksgrenadier* Division: *Generalmajor* Erich Seidel
11 Panzer Division: *Generalleutnant* Wend von Wietersheim
3 Panzergrenadier Division: *Generalleutnant* Walter Denkert
6.*SS-Gebirgs-Division*: *SS-Gruppenführer* Karl-Heinrich Brenner
10.SS Panzer Division: *SS-Brigadeführer* Heinz Harmel

5.Panzer-Armee

General der Panzertruppen Hasso Eccard von Manteuffel (9 Sep. 1944–8 Mar. 1945)
Chef: *Generalmajor* Wagner
Units:
9 *FlaK* Brigade: *Oberst* Paul Schluchtmann; Ia: *Hauptmann* Helmut Graf
1 *FlaK Sturm* Regiment
182 *FlaK* Regiment
Volks-Artillerie-Korps 410
Führer-Begleit Brigade: *Oberst* Bremer

XXXXVII Panzer-Korps

General der Panzertruppen Freiherr Heinrich von Lüttwitz
Panzer-Lehr Division
Generalleutnant Fritz Bayerlein
Panzergrenadier Regiment 901: *Oberst*
Scholze Panzergrenadier Regiment 902: *Oberst* Gutmann
Panzer Regiment 130
Panzer-Artillerie-Regiment 130: *Oberst* Luxenberger
Panzer-Aufklarungs-Abteilung 130: Major von Born-Fallois
Panzer-FlaK-Artillerie-Abteilung 311
Panzerjäger-Abteilung 130
Panzer-Pionier-Bataillon 130: Major Brandt
Panzer-Nachrichten-Abteilung 130
26 *Volksgrenadier* Division
Generalmajor Heinz Kokott
9 Panzer Division
Generalleutnant Freiherr von Harald Elverfeldt
15 Panzergrenadier Division
Generalmajor Hans-Joachim Deckert
182 *FlaK* Regiment

XXXXIX Panzer-Korps

General der Panzertruppen Karl Decker
167 *Volksgrenadier* Division
Generalleutnant Hanskurt Hocker
1.SS-Panzer-Division (28.12.1944)
SS-Brigadeführer Wilhelm Mohnke
10.SS-Panzer-Division (13.01.1945)
SS-Brigadeführer Heinz Harmel
7 *Fallschirmjäger* Division (13.01.1945)
Generalleutnant Wolfgang Erdmann
StuG Brigade 394 (01.13.1945)
StuG-Artillerie Brigade 667 (13.01.1945)

LVIII Armee-Korps

General der Panzertruppen Walter Kruger
560 *Volksgrenadier* Division (assigned to LXVI *Armee-Korps* on 24 Dec. 1944)
Commander: *Generalmajor* Rudolf Bader
116 Panzer Division
Commander: *Generalmajor* Siegfried von Waldenburg
2 Panzer Division Commander: *Generalmajor* Meinrad von Lauchert

LXVI Armee-Korps

(assigned to 6.*Panzer.Armee* on 24 Dec. 1944)

Commander: *General der Artillerie* Walther Lucht
18 *Volksgrenadier* Division
Commander: *Generalmajor* Günther Hoffman-Schönborn
62 *Volksgrenadier* Division
Commander: *Generalmajor* Fritz Warnecke
Führer-Begleit-Brigade (assigned on 18 Dec. 1944)

6.Panzer-Armee

SS-Oberstgruppenführer Josef 'Sepp' Dietrich
Chef: *SS-Brigadeführer* Fritz Kraemer
Ia: *SS-Obersturmbannführer* Georg Mayer
Ib: *SS-Oberführer* Herbert Ewert
O1: *SS-Untersturmführer* Kurt Sommer
IIa: *Oberstleutnant* (H.) Dittman
Units:
Skorzeny Brigade 150: Commander *SS-Obersturmbannführer* Otto Skorzeny
Volks-Artillerie-Korps 388/402/405
Volks-Werfer-Brigade 4/9/17
2 *FlaK* Division: Commander *Oberst* Fritz Laicher
246 *Volksgrenadier* Division (reserve for *Armee*, 19.12.1944);
    Commander: *Generalmajor* Peter Körte

LXVII Armee-Korps

Commander: *General der Infanterie* Otto Hitzfeld
272 *Volksgrenadier* Division; Commander: *Generalleutnant* Eugen König
326 *Volksgrenadier* Division; Commander: *Generalmajor* Dr Erwin Kaschner
2 *FlaK-Sturm-Regiment*

LXVI Armee-Korps

Commander: *General der Artillerie* Walther Lucht
12 *Volksgrenadier* Division; Commander: *Generalleutnant* Gerhard Engel
62 *Volksgrenadier* Division; Commander: *Generalmajor* Fritz Warnecke
560 *Volksgrenadier* Division; Commander: *Generalmajor* Rudolf Bader

Korps Felber

Commander: *General der Infanterie* Hans Felber
18 *Volksgrenadier* Division (1.1.45 attached); Commander: *Generalmajor* Günther
    Hoffman-Schönborn

62 *Volksgrenadier* Division (1.1.45 attached); Commander: *Generalmajor* Fritz Warnecke

I.SS-Panzer-Korps

SS-Gruppenführer Hermann Priess
Chef: *SS-Obersturmbannführer* Rudolf Lehmann
Ia: *SS-Sturmbannführer* Erich Maas
Ib: *SS-Standartenführer* Werner Reimer
Ic: *SS-Hauptsturmführer* Ekkehart Eckert
IIa: *SS-Sturmbannführer* Hermann Weiser
Units:
277 *Volksgrenadier* Division: *Generalmajor* Wilhelm Viebig (with attached)
I./SS-Panzergrenadier Regiment.25; Commander: *SS-Hauptsturmführer* Ott
12 *Volksgrenadier* Division: *Generalleutnant* Gerhard Engel (assigned to LXVI *Armee-Korps* on 24 Dec. 1944)
Grenadier Regiment.48: *Oberstleutnant* Wilhelm Osterhold
Grenadier Regiment.89: *Oberstleutnant* Gerhard Lemcke
Füsilier-Regiment.27: *Oberstleutnant* Heinz-Georg Lemm
3 *FlaK-Sturm-Regiment*
4 *FlaK-Sturm-Regiment*
340 *Volksgrenadier* Division: *Generalleutnant* Theodore Tolsdorff (assigned to Korps on 12.01.1945)
3 *Fallschirmjäger* Division; Commander: *Generalmajor* Walther Wadehn (with two companies from *SS-Pionier.Bataillon* LSSAH)
1.SS Panzer Division
SS-Brigadeführer Wilhelm Mohnke
Ia: *SS-Sturmbannführer* Ralf Tiemann
Ib: *SS-Hauptsturmführer* Stegemann
Ic: *SS-Hauptsturmführer* Hans Bernhard
O1: *SS-Hauptsturmführer* Kurt Brüning
IIa: *SS-Hauptsturmführer* Meyer
(*Kampfgruppe Knittel*): 16 Dec. 1944
Stabskompanie; Commander: *SS-Obersturmführer* Goltz
2.kp.: *SS-Obersturmführer* Coblenz
3.kp.: *SS-Obersturmführer* Leidreiter
4.kp.: *SS-Obersturmführer* Wagner
Vers.Kompanie: *SS-Obersturmführer* Reuss
2./SS-Panzer.Pionier.Abteilung.1: *SS-Untersturmführer* Unglaube
2./SS-Panzer.Artillerie.Regiment.1: *SS-Obersturmführer* Butschek

12.SS Panzer Division

SS-Brigadeführer Hugo Kraas

Ia: *SS-Obersturmbannführer* Hubert Meyer

Ib: *SS-Obersturmbannführer* Buchsein

Ic: *SS-Obersturmbannführer* Doldi

O1: *SS-Hauptsturmführer* Reitzenstein

IIa: *SS-Hauptsturmführer* Hofler

Schwere-Panzerjäger-Abteilung 559 (Temp)

Schwere-Panzerjäger-Abteilung 560: Major Streger (attached to division)

Divisionsbegleitkompanie: *SS-Untersturmführer* Stier

SS Panzer Regiment 12: *SS-Sturmbannführer* Kuhlmann; Adjutant: *SS-Obersturmführer*
    Ribbentrop

I.Abteilung: *SS-Sturmbannführer* Jurgensen, KIA 23.12.1944, then *SS-Obersturmführer*
    Ribbentrop

1–4 kp.

II.Abteilung: *SS-Hauptsturmführer* Seigel

5–9 kp.

SS Panzergrenadier Regiment 25; Commander: *SS-Sturmbannführer* S. Müller

Attached to the regiment on 27/28 Dec.:

SS-Panzer.Aufklärungs.Abteilung.2 Das Reich: *SS-Sturmbannführer* Ernst Krag

9(Arm)./SS Panzergrenadier Regiment 4 *Der Führer*

III./SS-Panzer.Artillerie.Regiment.2 Das Reich: *SS-Hauptsturmführer* Herbert Hoffman

Divisionssturmkompanie

I.Bataillon; Commander: *SS-Hauptsturmführer* Ott; Adjutant: *SS-Obersturmführer* Klein

1–4 kp.

II.Bataillon: *SS-Obersturmbannführer* Schulze, then *SS-Hauptsturmführer* Damsch

5–8 kp.

III.Bataillon: *SS-Hauptsturmführer* Bruckner; Adjutant: *SS-Untersturmführer* Schauble

9–12 kp.

SS Panzergrenadier Regiment 26; Commander: *SS-Sturmbannführer* Krause;
    Adjutant: *SS-Obersturmführer* Holzl

I.Bataillon: *SS-Hauptsturmführer* Hein; Adjutant: SS-Untersturmführer Bergmann

1–4 kp.

II.Bataillon: *SS-Hauptsturmführer* Hauschild; Adjutant: *SS-Obersturmführer* Lubbe

5-8 kp.

III.Bataillon: *SS-Hauptsturmführer* Urabl; Adjutant: *SS-Obersturmführer* Kugler

9–12 kp. (attached to battalion on 16.12.1944, was 1./SS-Pionier.Bataillon.12)

SS-Werfer-Abteilung 12: SS W. Müller; Adjutant: *SS-Obersturmführer* Lammerhirt

1–4 *Batterie*

SS-FlaK-Abteilung 12: *SS-Sturmbannführer* Dr Loenicker; Adjutant: *SS-Untersturmführer*
    Kolb

1–5 *Batterie*

SS-Aufklarungs-Abteilung 12: *SS-Sturmbannführer* Bremer

1–5 kp.

SS-Artillerie-Regiment 12: *SS-Obersturmbannführer* Drexler; Adjutant:
   SS-Hauptsturmführer Macke

I.Abteilung: *SS-Sturmbannführer* Müller

1–3 *Batterie*

II.Abteilung attached to III./Panzergrenadier.25

III.Abteilung: *SS-Hauptsturmführer* Fritsch; Adjutant: *SS-Untersturmführer* Wirisch

7–10 *Batterie*

SS-Panzerjäger-Abteilung 12: Commander: *SS-Hauptsturmführer* Brockschmidt;
   Adjutant: *SS-Untersturmführer* Protst

1–3 kp.

Kampfgruppe Zeine

1./Panzerjäger.Abteilung.12: *SS-Obersturmführer* Zeine

Three *Panzerjägers* with one infantry zug

Kampfgruppe Kuhlmann

19/20 Dec. 1944

Staff of Panzer Regiment 12

I./Panzergrenadier Regiment 26: *SS-Sturmbannführer* Hein

*II./Artillerie.Regiment.*12: *SS-Sturmbannführer* Neumann

Schwere Panzerjäger Abteilung 560: Major Streger

From 28.12.1944 to 31.12.1944 I.SS Panzer Korps was under the 5.*Panzer-Armee*
   and from 01.01.1945 to 12.01.1945 was also under the 5.*Panzer-Armee* with the
   9 and 12 SS Panzer Divisions and 340 *Volksgrenadier* Division

II.SS-Panzer-Korps

SS-Obergruppenführer Wilhelm Bittrich

Chef: *SS-Obersturmbannführer* Baldur Keller

Ia: Major (H.) Schiller

Ib: *SS-Sturmbannführer* Hans Keppler

Ic: *SS-Hauptsturmführer* Hans-Wedigo von le Coq

O1: *SS-Hauptsturmführer* Fritz Galleitner

IIa: *SS-Sturmbannführer* Wolfgang Ollrog

2.SS Panzer Division

SS-Brigadeführer Heinz Lammerding

Ia: *SS-Obersturmbannführer* Albert Stuckler

Ib: *SS-Sturmbannführer* Heino von Goldacker

Ic: *SS-Obersturmführer* Aurel Kowatsch

O1: *SS-Hauptsturmführer* Claudius Rupp

IIa: *SS-Hauptsturmführer* Otto Resch

9 SS Panzer Division (attached to the I.SS Panzer Korps on 01.01.1945)

SS-Oberführer Sylvester Stadler

Ia: *SS-Sturmbannführer* Emil Sturzbecker

Ib: *SS-Hauptsturmführer* Walter Uhlmann

Ic: *SS-Hauptsturmführer* Karl Doring

IIa: *SS-Sturmbannführer* Karl-Theodore Locquenghein

Attached to the division was *Schwere Panzerjäger Abteilung* 519

10 SS Panzer Division (attached to Korps on 25.12.1944)

SS-Brigadeführer Heinz Harmel

Ia: *SS-Sturmbannführer* Hans-Joachim Stolley

Ib: *SS-Sturmbannführer* Georg-Waldemar Rosch

Ic: *SS-Sturmbannführer* Walter Shorn

IIa: *SS-Sturmbannführer* Rudolf Reinecke

Schwere SS Panzerabteilung 102/502: *SS-Sturmbannführer* Kurt Hartrampf

SS-Werfer-Abteilung 102/502: *SS-Hauptsturmführer* Alfred Nickmann

560 V.G.D. attached to Korps on 31.12.44

116 Panzer Division attached to Korps on 01.01.1945

Attached to the Korps on 18 Dec. 1944:

12 SS Panzer Division

3 *Fallschirmjäger* Division

277 *Volksgrenadier* Division

3 Panzergrenadier Division

7.Armee

General der Panzertruppen Erich Brandenberger

Chef: *Oberst i.G.* Freiherr von Gersdorff

Units:

FlaK Regiment 15

LIII Armee Korps

General der Kavallerie Edwin Graf von Rotkirch und Trach

Security Battalions

Engineer Brigade 47

26 *Volksgrenadier* Division: *Generalmajor* Heinz Kokott (attached on 24/25 Dec. 1944)

9 *Volksgrenadier* Division: *Generalmajor* Werner Kolb (attached on 27 Dec. 1944)

79 *Volksgrenadier* Division: *Generalmajor* Alois Weber (attached on 13 Jan. 1945)

167 *Volksgrenadier* Division: *Generalleutnant* Hanskurt Hocker (reserve on 16 Dec., with Korps on 22 Dec.)

276 *Volksgrenadier* Division: *Generalmajor* Hugo Dempwolf (attached on 13 Jan. 1945)
5 *Fallschirmjäger* Division: *Generalmajor* Sebastian Ludwig Heilmann (attached on 25 Dec. 1944)
1 *FlaK* Brigade (attached on 25 Dec. 1944)
Führer-Grenadier-Brigade (attached on 25 Dec. 1944)

LXXXV Armee Korps

General der Panzertruppen Smilo Freiherr von Lüttwitz
352 *Volksgrenadier* Division: General Richard Bazing
5 *Fallschirmjäger* Division: *Generalmajor* Sebastian Ludwig Heilmann

15.Armee

General der Infanterie Gustav-Adolf von Zangen
Units:
1 *FlaK* Brigade: *Oberst* Oskar Schottl (assigned to LIII A.K. on 25 Dec. 1944)
Schwere Panzerabteilung 506: Major Lange
FlaK Regiment 18

XII.SS-Armee Korps

General der Infanterie Gunther Blumentritt
Chef: *Oberst* Ulrich Ulms
Ia: Major Karl-Georg Reuther
Ib: *SS-Hauptsturmführer* Heinrich Barner
Ic: Major Fritz Janssen
IIa: *SS-Sturmbannführer* Helmut Herzig
183 *Volksgrenadier* Division; Commander: *Generalleutnant* Wolfgang Lange
176 *Volksgrenadier* Division; Commander: *Generalmajor* Christian-Johannes Landau
59 *Volksgrenadier* Division; Commander: *Generalleutnant* Walter Poppe
Volks-Artillerie-Korps 407: *Oberst* Hermann Seidel
Korps Felber (assigned to 6.*Panzer Armee* on 1 Jan. 1945)
340 *Volksgrenadier* Division: *Generalleutnant* Theodore Tolsdorff

LXXXI Armee Korps

General der Infanterie Friedrich Kochling
363 *Volksgrenadier* Division: *Generalleutnant* August Dettling
246 *Volksgrenadier* Division: *Generalmajor* Peter Korte (attached to Korps until 17 Dec. 1944)
47 *Volksgrenadier* Division: *Generalleutnant* Max Bork
Korps attachments:
Volks-Artillerie-Korps 409: *Oberstleutnant* Willibald Neudecker

Schwere Panzerabteilung 301: *Hauptmann* Kramer
Panzer Abteilung 319
StuG Brigade 341
Schwere Panzerabteilung 682

LXXIV Armee Korps

General der Infanterie Karl Puchler
353 Infantry Division: *Generalleutnant* Paul Mahlmann
85 Infantry Division: *Generalmajor* Helmut Bechler
89 Infantry Division: *Generalmajor* Walter Burns
Korps attachments:
StuG Brigade 394: *Hauptmann* Gert Schmock
344 Infantry Division (only the artillery was used; the division was pulled out of the Ardennes on 29 Dec. 1944)

Kampfgruppe Peiper

SS-Panzer Regiment 1 LSSAH
SS-Obersturmbannführer Joachim Peiper
Adjutant: *SS-Hauptsturmführer* Hans Gruhle/*SS-Untersturmführer* Arndt Fischer
Panther 001 (J. Peiper's):
Driver: *Oberscharführer* Otto Becker
Loader: *Sturmmann* Wilhelm Nasshag
Gunner (not known)
Radio-Operator: *Rottenführer* Paul Schierig
I./SS Panzer Regiment 1: *SS-Sturmbannführer* Werner Poetschke
HQ Company, I./SS Panzer Regiment 1: SS Rolf Buchheim
Supply Company, I./SS Panzer Regiment 1: SS Ernst Otto
1./SS Panzer Regiment 1: *SS-Obersturmführer* Karl Kremser
2./SS Panzer Regiment 1: *SS-Obersturmführer* Friedrich Christ
6./SS Panzer Regiment 1: *SS-Obersturmführer* Benoni Junker
Schwere SS-Panzer-Abteilung 501; Commander: *SS-Obersturmbannführer* Heinz von Westernhagen
Tiger 007; Adjutant: *SS-Untersturmführer* Eduard Kalinowsky, Tiger 008
Supply Company: *SS-Panzer.Abteilung.501*; *SS-Obersturmführer* Paul Vogt
1./*SS Panzer.Abteilung.501*: *SS-Obersturmführer* Jurgen Wessel, Tiger 105
2./*SS Panzer.Abteilung.501*: *SS-Hauptsturmführer* Rolf Mobius, Tiger 205
3./*SS Panzer.Abteilung.501*: *SS-Hauptsturmführer* Heinz Birnschein
7./SS Panzer Regiment 1: *SS-Hauptsturmführer* Oskar Klingelhofer
9./SS Panzer Regiment 1: *SS-Obersturmführer* Erich Rumpf
10.(*FlaK*)/SS Panzer Regiment 1: *SS-Obersturmführer* Karl-Heinz Vogler

Maintenance Company, SS Panzer Regiment 1: *SS-Obersturmführer* Wilhelm
Ratschko

III.(gep)/SS Panzergrenadier Regiment 2: *SS-Hauptsturmführer* Josef Diefenthal

9.(gep)/SS Panzergrenadier Regiment 2: *SS-Ubersturmführer* Max Leike

10.(gep)/SS Panzergrenadier Regiment 2: *SS-Obersturmführer* Georg Preuss

11.(gep)/SS Panzergrenadier Regiment 2: *SS-Obersturmführer* Heinz Tomhardt

12.(gep)/SS Panzergrenadier Regiment 2: *SS-Hauptscharführer* Jochen Thiele

4.(leichte)/*SS Panzer.Abteilung.501*: *SS-Hauptsturmführer* Wilhelm Spitz

Supply company, III./SS Panzergrenadier Regiment 2: *SS-Obersturmführer* Wolfgang
Ludecke

13.(IG)/SS Panzergrenadier Regiment 2: *SS-Obersturmführer* Koch

3.(gep)/*SS-Panzer.Pionier.Bataillon*.1: *SS-Obersturmführer* Franz Sievers

FlaK Abteilung 84: Major von Sacken

1–4 Batterie

Fallschirmjäger Regiment 9: *Oberst* von Hoffmann

I./*Regiment.9*: *Hauptmann* Fritz Schiffke

II./*Regiment.9*: Major Taubert

Kampfgruppe Krag

16 Dec. 1944

SS-Panzer-Aufklarungs-Abteilung 2 (*SS-Sturmbannführer* Ernst Krag)

2./SS-Sturmgeschütz-Abteilung

1./SS-Panzer-Pionier-Bataillon 2

I./SS-Panzer-Artillerie-Regiment 2 (*SS-Hauptsturmführer* Herbert Hoffman)

One Medical Support Zug